INTRODUCTION TO HDL-BASED DESIGN USING

VHDL

STEVE CARLSON

SYNOPSYS INC.

Design Compiler, HDL Compiler, VHDL
Compiler, Library Compiler, and
RoundTrip VHDL Synthesis are
trademarks of Synopsys Inc. Synopsys
and the Synopsys logo are registered
trademarks of Synopsys Inc.

Synopsys Inc.
700 East Middlefield Road
Mountain View, CA 94043-4033
415.962.5000 or 800.541.7737

Acknowledgments

Synopsys began its all-out assault on a VHDL implementation in the spring of 1989. A number of important luminaries helped to shape the VHDL synthesis capability offered today. We wish to express our thanks to Larry Saunders of IBM, Ron Waxman of the University of Virginia, Paul Hunter of the Navy, Jim Armstrong of Virginia Tech., and John Hines of the Air Force for their suggestions, thoughtful criticism, and encouragement on our VHDL plan.

The production of this book was truly a team effort. The core of the product development team is responsible for most of the ideas contained in this work. That team consists of Emil Girczyc, Brent Gregory, Jerry Huth, Bill Krieger, and Russ Segal. The examples in Chapters 3 and 4 were prepared by Brent Gregory and Russ Segal; the original 2910 code of Chapter 6 was written by Bill Krieger.

Applications support for this project was provided by Deirdre Hanford, Pratap Reddy, Stephan Andres, and T.J. Boer.

The preparation of this book was completed through the sometimes excruciating efforts of Janet Greene, Lois Carroll, Franette Armstrong, and Ruby Karganilla.

Among the many reviewers of this work, were: Stan Mazor, Bob Smith, Aart de Geus, Dave Gregory, Rick Rudell, Antony Dennis, Pierre Wildman, Bob Dahlberg, Tom Daspit, Ken Scott, William Rohm, Patricia Langstraat, Ken Dickman, and Kurt Keutzer.

The UART example of Chapter 5 is based on the model described in Chapter 5 of "Chip-Level Modeling with VHDL" by James Armstrong and published by Prentice-Hall in 1989.

We also wish to express our gratitude to the gentlemen of the SM-ALC/MMETM group at McClellan Air Force Base and Rockwell International Autonetics Electronics Systems Division for their help in obtaining and completing the F-111 DSTU reprocurement project discussed in Chapter 7. Technical support was also provided by National Semiconductor and Texas Instruments on this project.

Steve Carlson
April, 1991

About this Book

This book is divided into seven chapters, each with a different focus:

Chapter 1
Introduction defines HDL synthesis, describes the HDL synthesis design methodology, and defines VHDL. Chapter 1 also presents the benefits of the HDL synthesis design methodology and VHDL.

Chapter 2
The VHDL Synthesis Policy gives an overview of the Synopsys Synthesis Policy; this policy contains the guidelines for a successful HDL design methodology.

Chapter 3
VHDL Synthesis Primer is an introduction to VHDL synthesis from a language constructs viewpoint. Chapter 3 illustrates basic VHDL syntax and gate-level structures generated from RTL (register transfer level) VHDL code.

Chapter 4
Hardware Synthesis Primer is an introduction to synthesis from a hardware design viewpoint. Chapter 4 illustrates basic VHDL syntax and gate-level structures generated from RTL (register transfer level) VHDL code.

Chapter 5
Clock & Timing Methods is an introduction to clocking scheme representation and timing considerations for the synthesis process.

Chapter 6
Synthesizing The AM2910A concentrates on the VHDL code, unit simulation, and optimization of each module of the 2910 to help you understand the contours of the Synthesis Policy.

Chapter 7
VHDL Extraction is a tutorial on the extraction capability in Synopsys' VHDL Compiler.

C O N T E N T S

1

Introduction

2

VHDL Synthesis Policy

3

VHDL Synthesis Primer

CONTENTS

4

Hardware Synthesis Primer

5

Clock and Timing Methods

CONTENTS

6

7

1

Introduction

This book is an introduction to a new design paradigm: HDL Design coupled with synthesis. HDLs (hardware description languages) provide designers with the ability to describe a design's architectural and functional characteristics at a more abstract level of representation than a traditional gate-level design methodology allows. Synthesis provides an automated mechanism to generate an optimized gate-level representation from an HDL description. This document examines how this new paradigm for ASIC design is being used today.

Although many HDLs exist, VHDL is emerging as an industry standard. The use of VHDL has been mandated for ASIC designs by the DoD, and has been adopted as an IEEE standard. VHDL is used as the source language for the examples included in this document. The examples and the accompanying discussion in this document should provide insight into the practical application of an HDL design methodology.

HDL Synthesis Defined

Benefits of HDL Synthesis Methodology

VHDL Defined

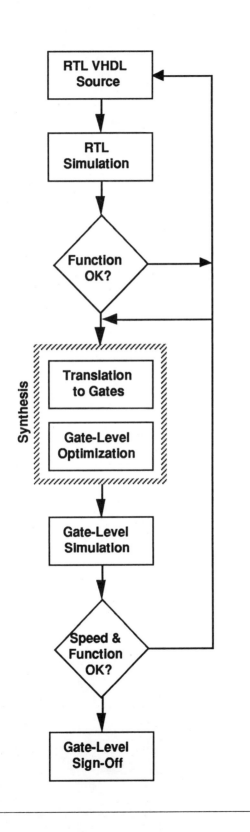

HDL Design Methodology

RTL VHDL Source

RTL Simulation

Function OK?

Synthesis

Translation to Gates

Gate-Level Optimization

Gate-Level Simulation

Speed & Function OK?

Gate-Level Sign-Off

What is HDL Synthesis?

Most simply stated, HDL synthesis is the process of turning an abstract text description of a design into gates (shown in the diagram at left). Synthesis is composed of two crucial elements:

Translation: Acts as the automated bridge between two levels of abstraction, in this case RTL and gate-level.

Optimization: Technology-specific design transformations to meet area and speed goals for the design.

An HDL design methodology encompasses the development of a design description, that description's validation, a synthesis step where the HDL description is transformed into an optimized gatelevel representation, and a final verification step. An important technology enabling this new design paradigm is synthesis; as shown at left, synthesis is at the heart of HDL design methodology.

The key to successful application of automatic synthesis technology is the use of a total design methodology that will yield predictable, accurate, and high quality results. To be successful, a design needs to meet the functional, area and timing goals of the project, and meet them on schedule. The methodology outlined in this document has numerous benefits that will enhance the success of any digital ASIC design team.

Synthesis Provides an Automated Link Between Levels of Abstraction

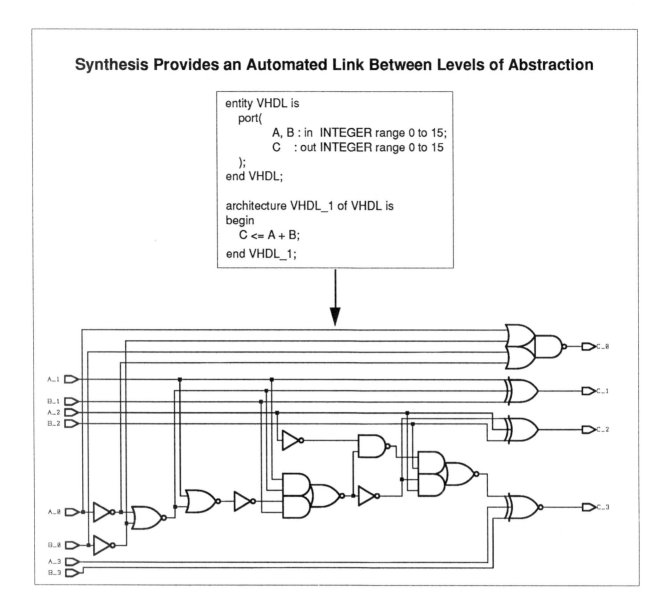

```
entity VHDL is
    port(
            A, B : in  INTEGER range 0 to 15;
            C    : out INTEGER range 0 to 15
    );
end VHDL;

architecture VHDL_1 of VHDL is
begin
    C <= A + B;
end VHDL_1;
```

Being able to predict the outcome of any process is fundamental to the most efficient use of that process. This is no less true for HDL synthesis, than for a semiconductor processing plant; just as junction depths must be highly predictable, so must the area and speed results of synthesis. Neither process can tolerate the cost and inefficiencies of sporadic results. For the HDL synthesis task we can measure "yield" in terms of the circuit quality with respect to a set of design goals. The two main ingredi-

ents of "high yield" synthesis are the input description and the optimization algorithms.

The input to HDL synthesis is an RTL (register transfer level) functional description of the network to be implemented. RTL descriptions are distinct from a behavioral level descriptions. The distinction is that *a behavioral description has no implied architecture in its representation*, while *an RTL level description has a definite, implied architecture*. The concept of synthesizing

3

Benefits of an HDL Synthesis Methodology

Why will this new methodology be the norm of tomorrow? The answer to this question is multidimensional, as the benefits of HDL design touch on all of the key areas of complex system design. Here are just of few of the compelling reasons to use HDL synthesis on your next project:

Designer productivity because designers are no longer required to manually enter gate-level descriptions, a great portion of the design implementation time is saved.

Design at a higher level of abstraction. Moving up to the RTL level allows more of the designers thinking to be at a conceptual level, rather than the gate level.

Improved design quality. The combination of automated optimization and the capability to quickly explore multiple design alternatives enables the designer to achieve higher quality final results.

Consistency between levels of abstraction. The pre- and post-synthesis network models are guaranteed to be equivalent because of the automated bridge between the RTL and gate levels.

Reduction of the silicon literacy requirement. The designer no longer need familiarize himself with the peculiarities of each ASIC vendor's libraries; technology specific aspects of design are automatic.

Technology-independent design. The high level descriptions are technology-independent, and thus retargetable, enabling the deferring or changing of vendor selection.

Facilitates design re-use because RTL descriptions are technology -independent and inherently easier to read than netlists, the re-use of design modules is much more practical.

an architecture from a behavioral description is still in an active area of research. Because of unpredictable resulting circuit quality, it will be some time before true behavioral-level synthesis can be applied in a production environment. However, RTL synthesis has proven itself in the industrial environment on numerous designs. An RTL description produces predictable results during the translation phase of synthesis.

The predictable results afforded by the translation phase of synthesis from an RTL description are not enough to ensure that design goals are met. Optimization performs the technology-specific network transformations to make the area speed trade-offs necessary to meet the design goals of a particular circuit. Optimization ensures that design quality is not being compromised for designer productivity; this is very important to fully realize the benefits of an HDL synthesis design methodology.

What is VHDL?

Actual development of VHDL by IBM, TI, and Intermetrics, began in 1983 under contract of the Department of Defense (DoD), and was finally ratified as IEEE Standard 1076 in 1987. The language adoption has been spurred along by the signing of MILSTD 454L, which requires all ASIC designs completed for DoD projects to be documented in VHDL.

VHDL is a strongly typed language with a rich set of constructs that enable the description of networks of widely varying complexity (systems, boards, chips, gates), at diverse levels of abstraction. The language constructs are generally broken into three levels of abstraction: behavioral, dataflow, and structural. Examples of each are shown at right.

The breadth of VHDL allows one language to be used for the entire design process. We will show how you can develop a working set of constructs to complete your ASIC design, just as you might choose a working set of gates when performing manual logic design.

As a company, Synopsys believes that VHDL is the catalyst that allows designers to move up to an HDL design methodology. The benefits described on the next page are attractive enough to cause a rapid adoption

Levels of Language Constructs

Behavioral constructs

```
architecture behavioral_view of full adder is
begin
  process
    variable N : integer;
    constant sum_vector : bit_vector (0 to 3) := "0101";
    constant carry_vector : bit_vector (0 to 3) := "0011";
  begin
    wait on X, Y, Cin;
    N := 0;
    if X = '1' then N := N + 1; end if;
    if Y = '1' then N := N + 1; end if;
    if Cin = '1' then N := N + 1; end if;
    Sum <= sum_vector(N) after 20 ns;
    Cout <= carry_vector(N) after 30 ns;
  end process;
end behavioral_view;
```

Data flow constructs

```
architecture dataflow_view of full adder is
  signal S : bit;
begin
  S <= X xor Y after 10 ns;
  Sum <= S xor Cin after 10 ns;
  Cout <= (X and Y) or (S and Cin) after 20 ns;
end dataflow_view;
```

Structural constructs

```
architecture structure_view of full adder is
  component half_adder port(I1,I2 : in bit; C,S : out bit);
    end component;
  component or_gate port(I1,I2 : in bit; O : out bit);
    end component;
  signal a,b,c : bit;
begin
  U1 : half_adder port map (X,Y,a,b);
  U2 : half_adder port map (c,Cin,c,Sum);
  U3 : or_gate port map (a,c,Cout);
end structure_view;
```

Benefits of VHDL for HDL Synthesis Design

The migration to VHDL is gaining momentum. Many benefits await the adopter of VHDL as the language of choice in an HDL synthesis design methodology:

Standard/Public language.
Because the language is a standard, designs are portable to alternate design environments.

One language for simulation and synthesis.
You need to learn only one language to complete the entire design task.

DoD compliance.
MILSTD 454 requires that all ASICs designed for government projects be documented in VHDL.

Models availability and portability.
Numerous sources of models in VHDL can be leveraged for new designs; using a standard permits model communication between vendors, contractors, and tool sets.

of VHDL as the design language of choice. If you wish to learn more about VHDL, refer to:

Synopsys VHDL Compiler Reference Manual, Synopsys Inc.

Synopsys VHDL Synthesis Workshop

IEEE Standard VHDL Language Reference Manual, IEEE STD-1076

VHDL: Hardware Description and Design, Roger Lipsett, et. al.

2

The VHDL Synthesis Policy

Design Methodology

Design Style

Supported Language Constructs

In this chapter is an introduction to the Synopsys HDL Synthesis Policy. After reading this chapter you should have a basic understanding of the principles of an HDL synthesis design methodology.

The Synopsys Synthesis Policy encompasses all of the elements necessary to ensure successful HDL synthesis. The purpose of the policy is to define a design methodology that enables you to predictably produce high quality silicon. This is important because the tremendous productivity gains afforded by an HDL synthesis methodology are lost if a high quality chip (in terms of both speed and area) is not the end result of the synthesis process. To address this issue we have developed a language-independent synthesis policy. The components to the policy are:

1. The design methodology
2. Templates for design description styles
3. The HDL vocabulary used to support the style and methodology

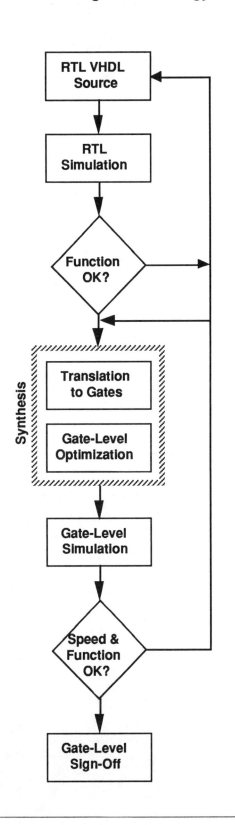

HDL Design Methodology

RTL VHDL Source

RTL Simulation

Function OK?

Synthesis

Translation to Gates

Gate-Level Optimization

Gate-Level Simulation

Speed & Function OK?

Gate-Level Sign-Off

Design Methodology

The design methodology guides the flow from an RTL (register transfer level) description down to an optimized gate-level description. This flow is shown in the diagram at left.

The HDL design process begins with the development of an RTL level functional description of the network to be implemented. The process of creating the RTL network description is often a two-tiered approach. The first steps involve a top-down architectural definition where all of the major functional units of the design are defined, and a top level design hierarchy is created. These units are typically ALU's, RAM, ROM, or data paths. The second steps are a bottom- up, or middle-up, functional description-creation process. In these steps, the source HDL describes the functional behavior characteristics of each one of the architectural units at an RTL level.

After the RTL descriptions have been completed, the validation process begins. Normally, the validation process proceeds in a bottom-up manner; each module is "unit-tested" to ensure desired operation. This is a simulation process where test stimuli are designed to test all of the module's functional behavior. After all the pieces of the design have been validated, the modules are assembled for a full validation of the design.

When a fully validated RTL design description is completed, then synthesis is ready to commence. In this phase of the design cycle the design is *translated* to a gate-level representation, and *optimized* with respect to a particular set of design goals and target technology library.

The results of the synthesis process is a technology specific, optimized gate-level representation. At this point a verification step takes place. Verification differs from validation. Validation is a proof by establishing a sufficient body of evidence, while verification is a proof by comparison between a validated description and a test description. The netlist should be simulated with the performance characteristics of the target silicon technology taken into consideration to verify that both the desired performance characteristics have been achieved, as well as the desired design functionality. If the specifications have not been met, then further optimization may be required, or possibly modifications to the RTL source must be made to try a new architecture that is more amenable to the design goals. If the gate-level description does meet the design objectives, then the designer proceeds through the normal ASIC house design submission path.

Design Style

The second component to the design policy is the style in which the HDL description is written. The style used for design description is a powerful way you can control the synthesis process. Similar to writing high-level software, different HDL descriptions of the same functionality can yield radically different networks. The power to control the synthesis process is the power to express the design intent. The resultant design quality comes from both the description style used by the engineer, and the power of the synthesis tool.

Chapter 4 of this book contains examples of typical hardware modules found in ASIC designs. These examples can be used as style templates for designing similar hardware. There are no strict style guidelines that need to be followed; rather, the examples represent description styles that have been found to be effective starting points for the synthesis process. The intent is to show, by way of example, proven styles of description for representative hardware types.

The areas in which the designer can exert the most influence using style as a control mechanism are in describing the sequential timing/clocking schemes, utilizing design hierarchy, and taking advantage of predefined blocks.

The timing/clocking schemes used in a design can drive the synthesis process to produce a more parallel or a more sequential design. From a high level, ASIC designs are typically thought of in terms of RAM, ROM, control, and data path elements. In turn, control and data path elements are composed of units such as ALUs, register files, state machines, and random logic. This level of decomposition provides the granularity of control to the designer to steer the synthesis process towards desired design goals.

Hierarchy is an important way that humans deal with complexity. It allows a complex problem to be partitioned into smaller, more manageable, problems. Hierarchy in digital design has importance beyond complexity management; it can impact the physical implementation of the design, the overall design quality, and has implications in design re-use. One of the great benefits of HDL synthesis is that the effects of creating and merging levels of hierarchy can be studied at relatively little cost. With a basic understanding of the ways in which hierarchy is used by the CAE tools downstream from synthesis (e.g., floorplanning and layout), you can use the synthesis process to arrive at a hierarchy that takes best advantage of those features.

Most ASIC design libraries have many large building blocks (multipliers, microcontrollers, etc.). These blocks are typically highly optimized for the particular technology being used, and provide the library user with a resource of high quality "parts" that might help in his design task. Synthesis tools, therefore, need to be able to cope with the inclusion of these blocks.

The most important point about style is that it provides a controlling mechanism to meet design objectives.

Supported Language Constructs

The third component of the Synopsys HDL Synthesis Policy is the language constructs used to support the level of description required for RTL synthesis. This is the designer's vocabulary for design description, the words that will form the design description style. An important distinction in the discussion of language support is the difference between the level of description at which a particular construct might be categorized, and the level of description used to describe the design. Constructs that are behavioral (e.g., the "+" operator) can be fully supported within the context of an RTL description, and will yield high quality circuits.

A problem that exists for synthesis tools is that most HDLs have been created for simulation and not specifically for synthesis. This is a problem only for synthesis tools and is actually a benefit for designers. The designer needs the capability to easily, in terms of both descriptive power and simulation turnaround time, validate each design description. Synthesis tools must be able to work around the simulation specific constructs of the language, and concentrate their efforts on those portions of the design description that relate to circuit function.

Following is a summary of the VHDL constructs supported for synthesis:

VHDL Constructs in V2.0 Synthesis Policy

Below are constructs supported as of this writing. Support continues to expand with advances in synthesis technology.

Fully-Supported Constructs

Package Declarations	Static Expressions
Package Bodies	If Statement
Constant Declaration	Case Statement
Simple Names	Next Statement
Operator Symbol	Return Statement
Logical Operators	Null Statement
Relational Operators	Attributes:
Signing Operators	RIGHT, HIGH, LOW,
Qualified Expression	BASE, LEFT, RANGE,
Type Conversion	LENGTH

Synthesis-Constrained Constructs:

Entity Declarations	Operator Overloading
Architecture Bodies	Miscellaneous Operators
Subprogram Declarations	Literals
Subprogram Bodies	Aggregates
Subprogram Overloading	Universal Expression
Function Call	Wait Statement
Resolution Functions	Signal Assignment State-
Libraries	ment
Enumeration Types	Array Variable Assign-
Integer Types	ment
Arrays	Procedure Call Statement
Records (release 2.1)	Loop Statement
Indexed Names	Exit Statement
Slice Names	Block Statement
Full Type Declaration	Process Statement
Subtype Declaration	Generate Statement
Signal Declaration	Concurrent Signal
Variable Declaration	Assign-
Interface Declaration	ment Statement
Component Declaration	Concurrent Procedure
Attribute Declaration	Call
Attribute Specification	Component Instantiation
Selected Names	Statement
Attribute Names	Package Standard
Addition Operators	Partially Supported
Multiplying Operators	Attributes:
	STABLE, EVENT
	REVERSE_RANGE(N)

Ignored Constructs:

Configuration Declarations	Access Types
Resolution Functions	FileTypes
Physical Types	File Declaration
Floating Point Types	Incomplete Type Declar-
	ation

Continued Over

VHDL Constructs in V2.0
Synthesis Policy
(continued)

Ignored Constructs (Continued)

Alias Declaration
Configuration Specification
Assertion Statement

Concurrent Assertion
Statement

Unsupported Constructs

Disconnection Specifica-
tion
Allocator
Context Information
Short-Circuit Operation
Package TEXTIO
Attributes:
POS(X), VAL(X)
SUCC(X), PRED(X)
LEFTOF(X), RIGHTOF(X)
LEFT(N),RANGE(N)

LENGTH(N)
DELAYED(T), QUIET(T)
TRANSACTION, ACTIVE
LAST_EVENT
LAST_ACTIVE
RIGHT(N), HIGH(N)
LOW(N), LAST_VALUE
BEHAVIOR
STRUCTURE

Synthesis Attributes

ARRIVAL, DRIVE
FALL_ARRIVAL
RISE_ARRIVAL
RISE_DRIVE
LOGIC_ONE
LOGIC_ZERO, EQUAL
OPPOSITE
DONT_TOUCH_NETWORK
LOAD, DONT_TOUCH
MAX_AREA
ENUM_ENCODING

MAX_TRANSITION
FALL_DRIVE
HOLD_CHECK
MAX_DELAY
MAX_RISE_DELAY
MIN_DELAY
MIN_FALL_DELAY
MIN_RISE_DELAY
UNCONNECTED
SETUP_CHECK

Synthetic Comments

SYNOPSYS_TRANSLATE_ON
SYNOPSYS_TRANSLATE_OFF
DC_SCRIPT_BEGIN
DC_SCRIPT_END
Other synthetic comments related to
resource sharing, state vector, compo-
nent implication, etc. (see 2.0 manual)

3

The VHDL Synthesis Primer

This **chapter** takes some of the mystery out of the VHDL synthesis process. It is organized as a collection of several small VHDL examples. These examples are constructed to illustrate how logic gates are synthesized from VHDL code; the entire chapter is presented from a language constructs viewpoint.

Each example consists of three parts. The first part is a small piece of VHDL source which contains only one or two VHDL constructs. This is followed by a short paragraph describing the VHDL code and how the code is synthesized. Finally, a schematic shows the synthesized logic once it has been mapped to a typical ASIC library.

Entities, Architectures

Bit Vectors, Sequential Statements

Packages, Component Instantiations

Arithmetic Operators

Comparison Operators

Array Indices

IF-Then-Else Statements

Case Statements, Enumerated Types

For Statements

Functions

Wait Statements

Generate Statements

Synthesis Attributes

Finite State Machine

Don't Cares and Three-State Inferencing

Entities and Architectures

```
entity VHDL is ──────────────          Entity and port declarations define interface
   port(
        A, B, C : in  BIT;
        Z      : out BIT
   );
end VHDL;


architecture VHDL_1 of VHDL is ──────  Architecture declaration defines implementation
begin
  Z <=  (A and B) or C; ────────────   Logic expression
end VHDL_1;
```

This example illustrates the synthesis of
VHDL's basic structural constructs. The
entity section defines the name of a VHDL
design. The port declarations declare a
signal interface to the design. The architecture section declares the body of the design
which, in this case, consists of simple logic.

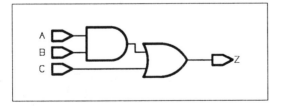

Bit Vectors and Sequential Statements

```
entity VHDL is
   port(
         A, B, C : in  BIT_VECTOR ( 1 to 5 );
         Z      : out BIT_VECTOR ( 1 to 5 )
   );
end VHDL;
```

Ports are 5 bits wide

```
architecture VHDL_1 of VHDL is
begin
   process (A, B, C)
```

Process groups sequential statements

```
      variable TEMP : BIT_VECTOR ( 1 to 5 );
```

Local variable

```
   begin
     TEMP := A and B;
     Z   <= TEMP or C;
   end process;
end VHDL_1;
```

Sequential statements

This example illustrates the use of VHDL's vectored data types. The synthesis tool will create multiple-bit busses for signals and variables whose types must be represented by more than one bit. This example also illustrates how VHDL processes may contain sequential statements that cause logic to be cascaded together (note the cascaded and-or structure).

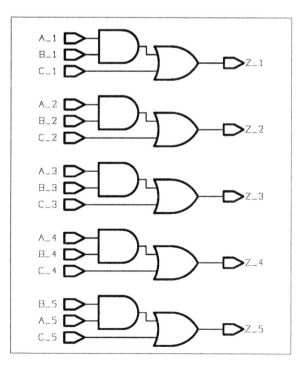

Packages and Component Instantiations

```
package cell_library is
```

Package holds external declarations

```
  component AN2          — 2 input AND
    port(A, B : in BIT; Z : out BIT);
  end component ;

  component EO           — 2 input XOR
    port(A, B : in BIT; Z : out BIT);
  end component ;
end cell_library;
```

Component declarations

```
use work.cell_library.all;
entity VHDL is
  port(
        A, B, C : in  BIT;
        Z      : out BIT
  );
end VHDL;
```

Makes package definitions usable in entity

```
architecture VHDL_1 of VHDL is
    signal AB : BIT;
begin
  U1: AN2 port map(A, B, AB);
  U2: EO  port map(AB, C, Z);
end VHDL_1;
```

Local signal declaration defines net

Structural component instances

This example illustrates how designers may synthesize from structural-level VHDL, and the use of a package (a VHDL package would normally be stored in a separate file). This style of VHDL may be used in conjunction with other tools that create VHDL netlist output. This example also illustrates the use of VHDL packages. You can also use packages to group together type and function declarations.

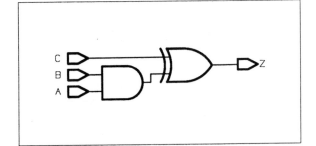

Arithmetic Operators

```
entity VHDL is
    port(
        A, B : in  INTEGER range 0 to 15;
        C    : out INTEGER range 0 to 15
    );
end VHDL;

architecture VHDL_1 of VHDL is
begin
    C <= A + B;
end VHDL_1;
```

Integer range defines number of bits in a port

Adding two integer values

This example illustrates synthesis support
for a higher-level arithmetic operator. The
arithmetic operators "+", "-" and abs operators are supported in their full generality.
Also "*", "/", "**", mod, and rem are also
supported for constant and power of 2
operands.

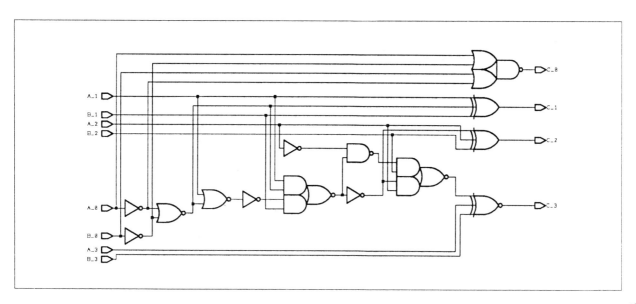

Comparison Operators

```
entity VHDL is
  port(
        A, B : in  INTEGER range 0 to 15;
        C    : out BOOLEAN
  );
end VHDL;

architecture VHDL_1 of VHDL is
begin
  C <= (A < B);
end VHDL_1;
```

Comparing two integer values

This example illustrates synthesis support for a comparison operator. Note the "<" sign in VHDL can imply a large amount of logic. The comparison operators "<", ">", "<=", ">=", "/=" and "=" operators are supported in their full generality.

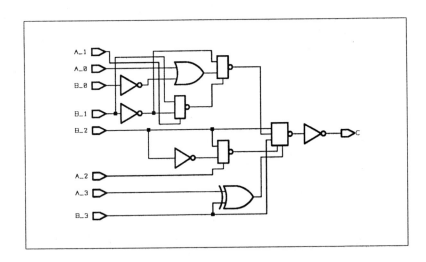

18

Array Indices

```
entity VHDL is
  port(
        A      : in BIT_VECTOR( 0 to 7 );
        OUTPUT : out BIT
  );
end VHDL;


architecture VHDL_1 of VHDL is
begin
  OUTPUT <= A( 5 );
end VHDL_1;
```

```
entity VHDL_VAR is
  port(
        A      : in BIT_VECTOR( 0 to 7 );
        INDEX  : in INTEGER range 0 to 7;
        OUTPUT : out BIT
  );
end VHDL;


architecture VHDL_1 of VHDL_VAR is
begin
  OUTPUT <= A( INDEX );
end VHDL_1;
```

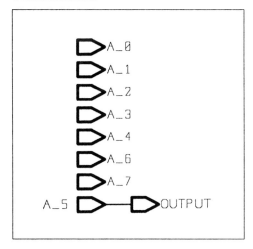

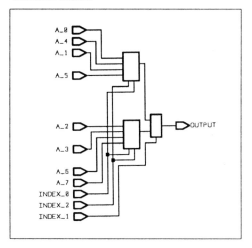

Select from array based on port input

This example illustrates the synthesis of indexed signals. Notice that there are two distinct cases considered. In the first example, the index is a constant. This is easily synthesized as a wire. In the second example the indexes may take on any value. A multiplexor of the correct size is synthesized to implement this construct.

If-Then-Else Statement

```
entity VHDL is
  port(
        A, B, USE_B : in Bit;
        Z    : out Bit);
end VHDL;
```

```
process (A, B, USE_B) begin
  if (USE_B = '1') then
   Z <= B;
  else
   Z <= A;
  end if;
 end process;
end VHDL_1;
```

If-then-else statement

The if-then-else statement is used in VHDL to conditionally execute sequential statements. For the purposes of synthesis, this statement implies a multiplexing of signals. Any signal or variable that is assigned to within the "if-then-else" will be multiplexed.

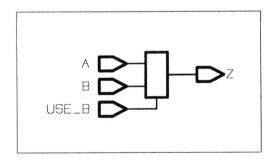

Case Statement and Enumerated Types

```
package types is

  type ENUM is (USE_A, USE_B, USE_C, USE_D);
  attribute ENUM_ENCODING of ENUM :
     type is "00 01 10 11";
end types;


use work.types.all;
entity VHDL is
  port(
        A, B, C, D  : in  BIT;
        CHOICE      : in  ENUM;
        Z           : out BIT
  );
end VHDL;


architecture VHDL_1 of VHDL is
begin
  process (CHOICE, A, B, C, D) begin
    case CHOICE is
      when USE_A =>  Z <= A;
      when USE_B =>  Z <= B;
      when USE_C =>  Z <= C;
      when USE_D =>  Z <= D;
    end case;
  end process;

end VHDL_1;
```

User-defined type (enumerated value).
Optionally supplied user encoding for type.

Case statement

This example illustrates the VHDL case
statement. Like the "if-then-else" statement,
case implies a multiplexer. This example
also illustrates the use of a user-defined type
(called ENUM). Note that a special synthesis attribute optionally specifies how the
user-defined type should be encoded in the
synthesized hardware.

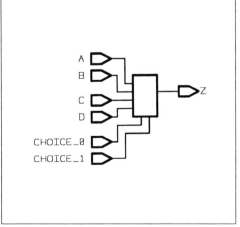

For Statements

```
entity VHDL is
   port(
         WORD   : in  BIT_VECTOR ( 0 to 7 );
         PARITY : out BIT
   );
end VHDL;

architecture VHDL_1 of VHDL is
begin
 process (word)
  variable RESULT : bit;
 begin
  RESULT := '0';

  for I in 0 to 7 loop
    RESULT := RESULT xor WORD(I);
  end loop;

  PARITY <= RESULT;
 end process;

end VHDL_1;
```

For loop to xor all bits in "WORD"

Assign result to output

The VHDL "for" statement may be used to iterate sections of logic. In this example, the for loop is used to create an 8-input exclusive or. The for loop is generally useful for creating custom adders, comparators, and other regular structures.

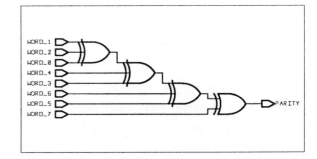

Functions

```
package ops is
  subtype WORD is BIT_VECTOR (1 to 16); ──────────  Subtype declaration
  function asr(INPUT : WORD) return WORD; ──────────  Function declaration
end ops;


package body ops is
  -- Arithmetic shift right function
  function asr(INPUT : WORD) return WORD is ──────────  Function body
    variable RESULT : WORD;
  begin
    RESULT(1)      := INPUT(1);
    RESULT(2 to 16) := INPUT(1 to 15); ──────────  Use of array "slices"
    return RESULT;
  end;
end ops;


use work.ops.all;
entity VHDL is
  port(
        INPUT  : in  WORD;
        OUTPUT : out WORD
  );
end VHDL;


architecture VHDL_1 of VHDL is
begin
  OUTPUT <= asr(asr(asr(INPUT)));       Function called multiple times
end VHDL_1;
```

This example illustrates several VHDL constructs, including subtypes, slices, and functions. The synthesizer will create hardware for a function whenever that function is called. Functions can be called several times and can be nested. Recursion, bounded by a constant, is also supported.

23

Wait Statements

```
entity VHDL is
  port(
        ENABLE : in  BIT;
        CLOCK  : in  BIT;
        TOGGLE : buffer BIT
  );
end VHDL;

architecture VHDL_1 of VHDL is
begin
  process begin
    wait until CLOCK'event and CLOCK='1';
    if (ENABLE = '1') then
      TOGGLE <= not TOGGLE;
    end if;
  end process;
end VHDL_1;
```

Wait statement infers a flip-flop

The use of a wait statement implies to the
synthesis tool that the value of signals must
be stored. Registers are inserted wherever
they required to create hardware whose
behavior matches the VHDL description. In
this example, the value of the signal
TOGGLE is preserved between clock cycles.

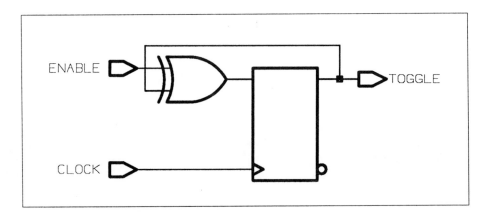

Generate Statements

```
--
-- GENERATE Version of single stack storage element
--
use work.SYNOPSYS.all;
use work.AMD_PACK.all;

entity STACK_ELEMENT is
  port( VALUE, CLOCK, WRITE_ENABLE,
      OUTPUT_ENABLE: in ADDRESS;
      OUTPUT: out ADDRESS);
end STACK_ELEMENT;

architecture STACK_ELEMENT_HDL of
STACK_ELEMENT is
  -- Three-state element from target library
  component BTS5 port(A: in BIT; E: in BIT; z: out BIT);
      end component;
  signal GATED_CLOCK: BIT;
  signal LATCHED_VALUE : ADDRESS;

begin
  -- make gated clock for flip-flop
  GATED_CLOCK <= CLOCK and WRITE_ENABLE;
  -- make flip-flop
  process
  begin
   wait until (not GATED_CLOCK'stable and
     GATED_CLOCK = '1');
   LATCHED_VALUE <= VALUE;
  end process;

  -- Three-state the output
  GEN_STACK : for I in ADDRESS_SIZE'LOW to
ADDRESS_SIZE'HIGH generate ──────────────    Generate address width of three-state drivers
   U1: BTS5 port map(LATCHED_VALUE(I),
     OUTPUT_ENABLE, OUTPUT(I));
  end generate;
end STACK_ELEMENT_HDL;
```

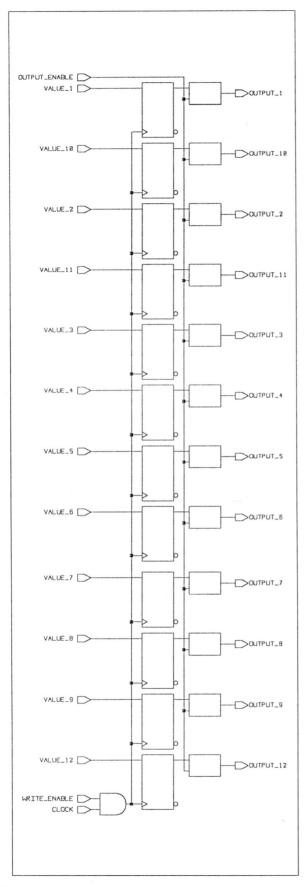

The generate statement is used to iteratively replicate a number of concurrent statements. The loop index can be used to customize each statement. The above example is taken from the Chapter 6 STACK_ELEMENT module, except for in this case the component instantiation of the three-state bus drivers has been completed via the generate statement. This example makes use of a number of the language constructs previously introduced as well as the generate statement. The generate statement should be thought of as a convenient shorthand notation for a series of similar concurrent statements.

Small

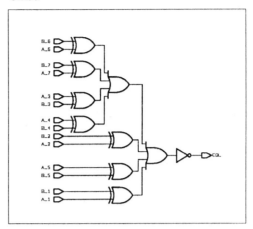

Synthesis Attributes

```
entity VHDL_SMALL is
  port(
        A, B : in  BIT_VECTOR (1 to 7);
        EQL  : out BOOLEAN
  );
end VHDL_SMALL;
```

```
architecture VHDL_SMALL_1 of VHDL_SMALL is
  attribute MAX_AREA of VHDL_SMALL : entity is 0;
begin
 EQL <=  (A = B);
end VHDL_SMALL_1;
```

Attribute controlling optimization: area constraint

```
entity VHDL_FAST is
  port(
        A, B : in  BIT_VECTOR (1 to 7);
        EQL  : out BOOLEAN
  );
end VHDL_FAST;
```

```
architecture VHDL_FAST_1 of VHDL_FAST is
  attribute MAX_DELAY of EQL : signal is 0;
begin
 EQL <=  (A = B);
end VHDL_FAST_1;
```

Attribute controlling optimization: delay constraint

Fast

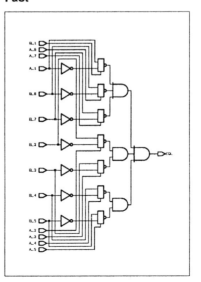

This example illustrates the use of synthesis attributes to control circuit optimization. In the VHDL_SMALL architecture, a MAX_AREA attribute causes the design to be optimized with a constrained area. In the VHDL_FAST architecture, a MAX_ DELAY attribute causes the design to be optimized with a constrained delay. Notice that both designs perform the same logical function. They simply have different performance characteristics.

Finite State Machine Example

```
package types is
   type ENUM is (STOP, SLOW, MEDIUM, FAST); ───────  ENUM declaration
end types;


use work.types.all;
entity VHDL is
   port(
         ACCELERATOR : in BIT;
         BRAKE      : in BIT;
         CLOCK      : in BIT;
         SPEED      : buffer ENUM ───────  Output is current state
   );
end VHDL;


architecture VHDL_1 of VHDL is
begin
  process begin
    wait until CLOCK'event and CLOCK = '1'; ───────  Implies state flip-flops
    if (ACCELERATOR = '1') then
      case SPEED is
          when STOP =>SPEED <= SLOW;
          when SLOW =>SPEED <= MEDIUM; ───────  Next state assignment based on input value
          when MEDIUM =>SPEED <= FAST;
          when FAST =>SPEED <= FAST;
      end case;
    elsif (BRAKE = '1') then
      case SPEED is
          when STOP =>SPEED <= STOP;
          when SLOW =>SPEED <= STOP;
          when MEDIUM =>SPEED <= SLOW;
          when FAST =>SPEED <= MEDIUM;
      end case;
    else
      -- Speed does not change
    end if;
  end process;
end VHDL_1;
```

This example brings together many of
constructs discussed earlier. Note that
VHDL constructs may be mixed arbitrarily
to create a complete design. It is also
interesting to note that the synthesized logic
has been optimized at the gate level. This
allows for a much more efficient design
than would be produced by simply cascading together translated constructs.

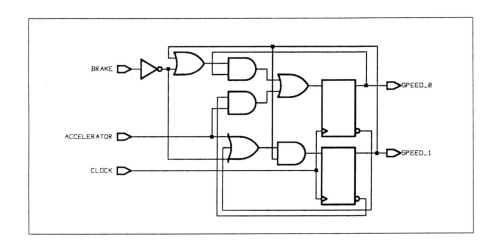

Don't Cares and Three-State Inferencing

```
use work.types.all;
entity UPPER_CONVERTER is
  port (BCD: in  MVL7_VECTOR(3 downto 0);
       LED: out MVL7_VECTOR(6 downto 0));
end UPPER_CONVERTER;

architecture BEHAVIORAL of UPPER_CONVERTER
is
  signal TMP : MVL7_VECTOR(6 downto 0);
begin
  process(BCD) begin
   case BCD is
    when "1010" => TMP <= "0011101";
    when "1011" => TMP <= "0011111";
    when "1100" => TMP <= "0001101";
    when "1101" => TMP <= "0111101";
    when "1110" => TMP <= "1001111";
    when "1111" => TMP <= "1000111";
    when others => TMP <= "XXXXXXX";
    end case;
   end process;

  process (BCD,TMP) begin
   if ((BCD(3) = '0') or
      (BCD(3) = '1' and BCD(2) = '0' and BCD(1) = '0'))
         then  LED <= TMP;
    else     LED <= "ZZZZZZZ";
    end if;
   end process;
  end BEHAVIORAL;
```

Assign to don't care value under appropriate conditions allows further optimization of logic

Assign to high impedance value under appropriate conditions tells tool where three-state logic is required

This example illustrates the specification of don't care conditions and the automatic inferencing of three-state logic. The function creates specific seven-segment display values for unused BCD values on a 4-bit bus (hex codes A-F). The specification of external don't care conditions allows further optimization of the network, and is very important in most partitioned designs. The method shown for three-state inferencing allows the user to specify three-state logic functions in a technology independent fashion.

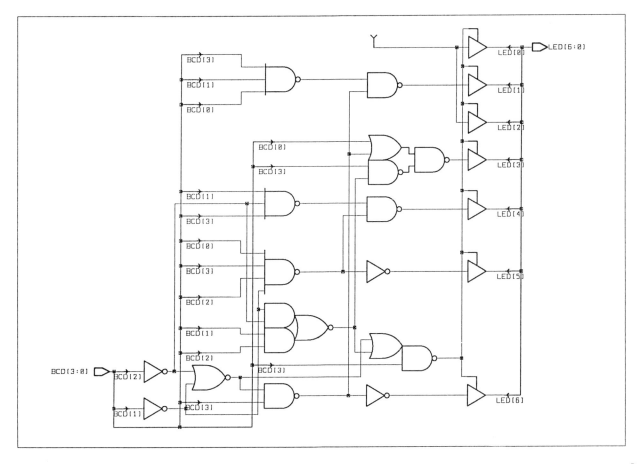

31

4

Hardware Synthesis Primer

This chapter continues where Chapter 3 left off, with hardware design examples. In contrast to the language construct oriented presentation of Chapter 3, this chapter looks at different classes of common hardware types.

As in Chapter 3, each example consists of three parts. The first part is a small piece of VHDL source which contains only one or two VHDL constructs. This is followed by a short paragraph describing the VHDL code and how the code is synthesized. Finally, a schematic shows the synthesized logic once it has been mapped to a typical ASIC library.

Moore Machine

Mealy Machine

ROM

Waveform Generators

Adder-Subtractor

Count Zeroes:
Combinational Version
Sequential Version

Drink Machine:
State Machine Version
Count Nickels Version

Carry Lookahead Adder

Serial-to-Parallel
Converters:
Counter and Shifter

PLA

Moore Machine

This example illustrates a basic Moore finite-state machine, summarized in the state diagram and state table below. The VHDL code to implement this finite-state machine follows. Note that the machine is described in two processes: one declares the synchronous elements of the design (registers); the other declares the combinational part of the design.

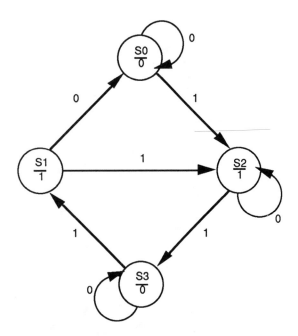

Present state	Next state		output (Z)
	x=0	x=1	
SO	SO	S2	0
S1	SO	S2	1
S2	S2	S3	1
S3	S3	S1	0

```
-- Moore machine                                    else
entity MOORE is                                       NEXT_STATE <= S2;
  port(X, CLOCK: in BIT;                            end if;
      Z: out BIT);                                  when S1 =>
end;                                                 Z <= '1';
                                                     if X = '0' then
architecture BEHAVIOR of MOORE is                      NEXT_STATE <= S0;
  type STATE_TYPE is (S0, S1, S2, S3);               else
  signal CURRENT_STATE, NEXT_STATE: STATE_TYPE;        NEXT_STATE <= S2;
begin                                                end if;
                                                     when S2 =>
  -- Process to hold synchronous elements (flip-flops)   Z <= '1';
  SYNCH: process                                     if X = '0' then
  begin                                                NEXT_STATE <= S2;
    wait until CLOCK'event and CLOCK = '1';           else
    CURRENT_STATE <= NEXT_STATE;                        NEXT_STATE <= S3;
  end process;                                        end if;
                                                     when S3 =>
  -- process to hold combinational logic.             Z <= '0';
  COMBIN: process(CURRENT_STATE, X)                   if X = '0' then
  begin                                                 NEXT_STATE <= S3;
    case CURRENT_STATE is                             else
      when S0 =>                                        NEXT_STATE <= S1;
        Z <= '0';                                     end if;
        if X = '0' then                             end case;
          NEXT_STATE <= S0;                         end process;
                                                  end BEHAVIOR;
```

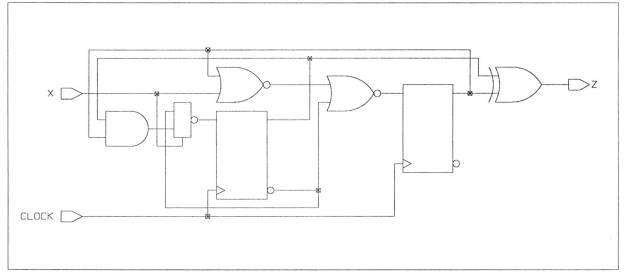

Mealy Machine

This example illustrates a basic Mealy finite-state machine, summarized in the following state diagram and state table. The VHDL code to implement this finite-state machine follows. It is described in two processes, as in the Moore Machine.

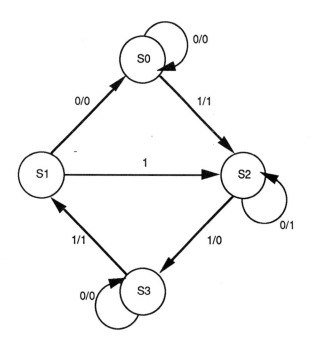

Present state	Next state		output (Z)	
	x=0	x=1	x=0	x=1
SO	SO	S2	0	1
S1	SO	S2	0	0
S2	S2	S3	1	0
S3	S3	S1	0	1

```
-- Mealy machine
entity MEALY is
  port(X, CLOCK: in BIT;
      Z: out BIT);
end;

architecture BEHAVIOR of MEALY is
  type STATE_TYPE is (S0, S1, S2, S3);
  signal CURRENT_STATE, NEXT_STATE:
STATE_TYPE;
begin

  -- Process to hold synchronous elements (flip-flops)
  SYNCH: process
  begin
    wait until CLOCK'event and CLOCK = '1';
    CURRENT_STATE <= NEXT-STATE;
  end process;


  -- process to hold combinational logic.
  COMBIN: process(CURRENT_STATE, X)
  begin
    case CURRENT_STATE is
      when S0 =>
      if X = '0' then
        Z <= '0';
        NEXT_STATE <= S0;
      else
        Z <= '1';
        NEXT_STATE <= S2;

      end if;
    when S1 =>
      if X = '0' then
        Z <= '0';
        NEXT_STATE <= S0;
      else
        Z <= '0';
        NEXT_STATE <= S2;
      end if;
    when S2 =>
      if X = '0' then
        Z <= '1';
        NEXT_STATE <= S2;
      else
        Z <= '0';
        NEXT_STATE <= S3;
      end if;
    when S3 =>
      if X = '0' then
        Z <= '0';
        NEXT_STATE <= S3;
      else
        Z <= '1';
        NEXT_STATE <= S1;
      end if;
    end case;
  end process;
end BEHAVIOR;
```

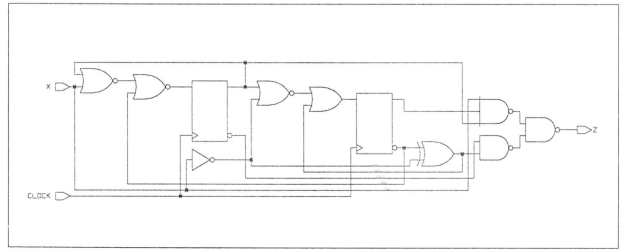

ROM (Read Only Memory)

This example illustrates how a ROM may be specified in VHDL. The ROM is specified as a array constant, ROM1. Each line of the constant specification defines the contents of one ROM address. To read from the ROM, simply index into the array. The number of storage locations and the ROM width can be specified as ROM parameters. The constant ROM1_WIDTH specifies that the ROM is 5 bits wide. The subtype ROM1_RANGE specifies that the ROM contains storage locations 0 to 7.

```
package ROMS is
  -- declare a 5x8 ROM called ROM1
  constant ROM1_WIDTH: INTEGER := 5;
  subtype ROM1_WORD is BIT_VECTOR (1 to ROM1_WIDTH);
  subtype ROM1_RANGE is INTEGER range 0 to 7;
  type ROM1_TABLE is array (0 to 7) of ROM1_WORD;
  constant ROM1: ROM1_TABLE := ROM1_TABLE'(
    "10101",              — ROM contents
    "10000",
    "11111",
    "11111",
    "10000",
    "10101",
    "11111",
    "11111");
end ROMS;

-- Entity that uses ROM1
use work.ROMS.all;
entity ROM is
  port(ADDR: in ROM1_RANGE;
       DATA: out ROM1_WORD);
end;
architecture BEHAVIOR of ROM is
begin
  DATA <= ROM1(ADDR);   — reading from the ROM
end BEHAVIOR;
```

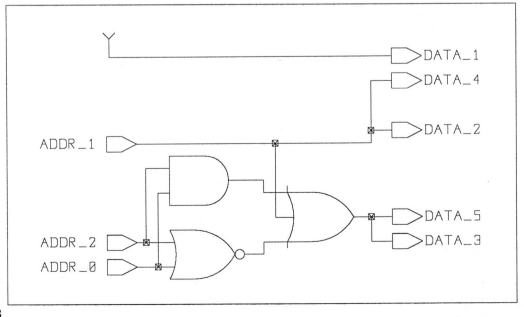

Once you have defined a ROM constant,
you may index into that constant many
times to read many values from the ROM.
If the ROM address is statically computable
(evaluates to a constant at analysis time),
then no logic is built. The appropriate data
value is simply inserted. If the ROM
address is not computable, then logic is
built for each index into the value. For this
reason, you should consider resource-
sharing when using a ROM. In the example, ADDR is not computable, so logic is
synthesized to compute the value.

The hardware the VHDL Compiler implements does not actually instantiate a typical
array-logic ROM, such as the ones available
from ASIC vendors. Instead, the ROM is
created from random logic gates (AND,
OR, NOT, etc.). This type of implementation is preferable for small or very regular
ROMs. For very large ROMs, you should
consider using an array-logic implementation that is supplied by your ASIC vendor.

Waveform Generator

This example illustrates how you can use the ROM of the previous example to implement a waveform generator. Assume you want to produce the waveform output shown in the figure below. First define a ROM which is wide enough to hold each of your output signals. Then define the ROM so that each time step is represented by an entry in the ROM. Then, create a counter which cycles through the addresses in the ROM, outputting one time step in the waveform at a time. This example shows an implementation for the waveform generator. It consists of a counter, a ROM, and some simple reset logic.

Note in the example at right that when STEP reaches the end of the ROM, it stops, outputting the last value, until a reset. To make the sequence automatically repeat, you need only change the line indicated by the comment to "STEP <= 0".

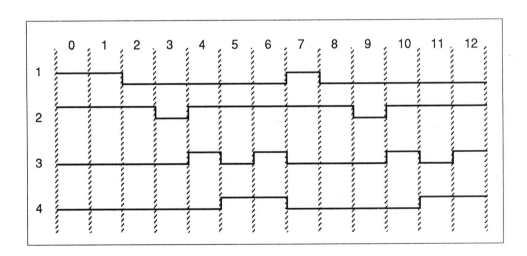

```
package ROMS is
  -- a 4x13 ROM called ROM1 that contains the
waveform
  constant ROM1_WIDTH: INTEGER := 4;
  subtype ROM1_WORD is BIT_VECTOR (1 to
            ROM1_WIDTH);
  subtype ROM1_RANGE is INTEGER range 0 to 12;
  type ROM1_TABLE is array (0 to 12) of
            ROM1_WORD;
  constant ROM1: ROM1_TABLE := ROM1_TABLE'(
    "1100",  -- time step 0
    "1100",  -- time step 1
    "0100",  -- time step 2
    "0000",  -- time step 3
    "0110",  -- time step 4
    "0101",  -- time step 5
    "0111",  -- time step 6
    "1100",  -- time step 7
    "0100",  -- time step 8
    "0000",  -- time step 9
    "0110",  -- time step 10
    "0101",  -- time step 11
    "0111"); -- time step 12
end ROMS;
```

```
-- Waveform generator
use work.ROMS.all;
entity WAVEFORM is
  port(CLOCK: in BIT;
      RESET: in BOOLEAN;
      WAVES: out ROM1_WORD);
end;

architecture BEHAVIOR of WAVEFORM is
  signal STEP: ROM1_RANGE;
begin

  TIMESTEP_COUNTER: process
  begin
    wait until CLOCK'event and CLOCK = '1';
    if RESET then              -- Detect reset
      -- restart
      STEP <= 0;
    elsif STEP = ROM1_RANGE'high then
      -- Have we finished?
      -- hold at last value
      STEP <= ROM1_RANGE'high;
      -- change this line to make sequence repeat.
    else
      -- continue cycling
      STEP <= STEP + 1;
    end if;
  end process;

  WAVES <= ROM1(STEP);
end BEHAVIOR;
```

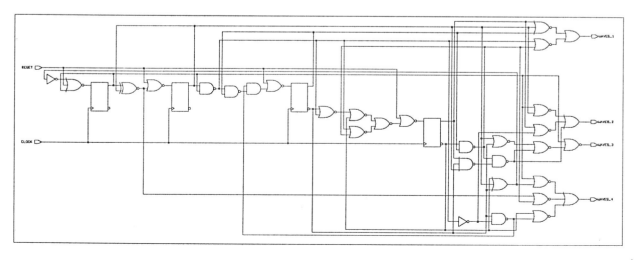

Smart Waveform Generator

The following example is an extension of the Waveform generator of the previous example. This "smart" waveform generator is capable of holding the waveform of any time step over several clock cycles. The figure above shows a waveform, similar to the waveform of the previous example, except several of the time steps are held for multiple clock cycles.

The implementation of the smart waveform generator is shown below. It is similar to the waveform generator of the previous example, but with two additions. A ROM, ROM2, has been added to hold the length of each time step. A value of 1 specifies that the corresponding time step should be 1 clock cycle long; a value of 80 specifies the time step should be 80 clock cycles long. The second addition to the previous waveform generator is a delay counter, that counts out the clock cycles between time steps.

```
package ROMS is
-- a 4x13 ROM called ROM1 that contains the waveform
constant ROM1_WIDTH: INTEGER := 4;
subtype ROM1_WORD is BIT_VECTOR (1 to
        ROM1_WIDTH);
subtype ROM1_RANGE is INTEGER range 0 to 12;
type ROM1_TABLE is array (0 to 12) of
        ROM1_WORD;
constant ROM1: ROM1_TABLE := ROM1_TABLE'(
   "1100",  -- time step 0
   "1100",  -- time step 1
   "0100",  -- time step 2
   "0000",  -- time step 3
   "0110",  -- time step 4
   "0101",  -- time step 5
   "0111",  -- time step 6
   "1100",  -- time step 7
   "0100",  -- time step 8
   "0000",  -- time step 9
   "0110",  -- time step 10
   "0101",  -- time step 11
   "0111");  -- time step 12

-- a 7x13 ROM called ROM2 that contains the delay
subtype ROM2_WORD is INTEGER range 0 to 100;
subtype ROM2_RANGE is INTEGER range 0 to 12;
type ROM2_TABLE is array (0 to 12) of ROM2_WORD;
constant ROM2: ROM2_TABLE :=
        ROM2_TABLE'(1,80,5,1,1,1,1,20,5,1,1,1,1);
end ROMS;
```

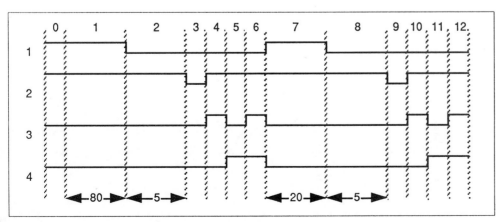

```vhdl
-- Smart Waveform Generator
use work.ROMS.all;
entity WAVEFORM is
  port(CLOCK: in BIT;
     RESET: in BOOLEAN;
     WAVES: out ROM1_WORD);
end;

architecture BEHAVIOR of WAVEFORM is
  signal STEP, NEXT_STEP: ROM1_RANGE;
  signal DELAY: ROM2_WORD;
begin

  -- Figure out the value of the next time step
  -- Make sure that NEXT_STEP does not go out of range.
  NEXT_STEP <= ROM1_RANGE'high when
          STEP = ROM1_RANGE'high else
          STEP + 1;

  -- Keep track of which time step we are in.
  TIMESTEP_COUNTER: process
  begin
    wait until CLOCK'event and CLOCK = '1';
    if RESET then            -- Detect reset
      -- restart
      STEP <= 0;
    elsif DELAY = 1 then
      -- continue cycling
      STEP <= NEXT_STEP;
```

```vhdl
    else
      -- wait for DELAY to count down
      -- do nothing here.
    end if;
  end process;

  -- Count the delay between time steps.
  DELAY_COUNTER: process
  begin
    wait until CLOCK'event and CLOCK = '1';
    if RESET then            -- Detect reset
      -- restart
      DELAY <= ROM2(0);
    elsif DELAY = 1 then
      -- Have we counted down?
      -- get next delay value
      DELAY <= ROM2(NEXT_STEP);
    else
      -- decrement the DELAY counter
      DELAY <= DELAY - 1;
    end if;
  end process;

  -- Output waveform value
  WAVES <= ROM1(STEP);
end BEHAVIOR;
```

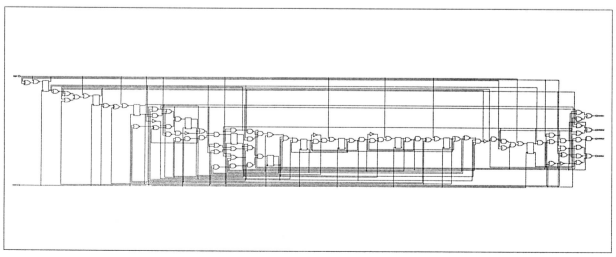

43

Parameterizable Adder-Subtracter

VHDL provides the capability for creating "parameterizable" functions. Parameterizable functions are functions which can be used for any size operands. This example shows a parameterized adder-subtracter. Note that the L and R arguments of the add_sub function are declared with the unconstrained array type BIT_VECTOR. When an unconstrained array type is used for an argument to a sub-program, the actual constraints of the array are taken from the values that are passed to the subprogram. In this example the arguments to the function, ARG1 and ARG2, are declared as "BIT_VECTOR(1 to 6)". This causes add_sub to work on 6-bit arrays.

Within the function add_sub, two temporary variables, A and B, are declared. These variables are created to be the same length as L and R, but have uniform constraints from "L'length-1 downto 0". By assigning arguments L and R to A and B, the array arguments are normalized to a known index range. Once the arguments are normalized, one can easily create a ripple-carry adder using a for loop.

Note that throughout the function add_sub, there are no explicit references to a fixed array length. Instead the VHDL attributes 'left and 'length are used. This allows the function to work on arrays of any length.

```
package MATH is
    -- add or subtract two BIT_VECTORs of the same length
    function add_sub(L, R: BIT_VECTOR; ADD: BOOLEAN)
                return BIT_VECTOR;
end MATH;

package body MATH is
    function add_sub(L, R: BIT_VECTOR; ADD: BOOLEAN)
                return BIT_VECTOR is
        variable carry: BIT;
        variable A, B, sum: BIT_VECTOR(L'length-1 downto 0);
    begin
        if ADD then
            -- set up for an add operation
            A := L;
            B := R;
            carry := '0';
        else
            -- set up for a subtract operation
            A := L;
            B := not R;
            carry := '1';
        end if;
```

```
        -- Create a ripple-carry chain and sum bits
        for i in 0 to A'left loop
            sum(i) := A(i) xor B(i) xor carry;
            carry := (A(i) and B(i)) or
                    (A(i) and carry) or
                    (carry and B(i));
        end loop;
        return sum;
    end;
end MATH;

use work.MATH.all;
entity test is
    port(ARG1, ARG2: in BIT_VECTOR(1 to 6);
        ADD: in BOOLEAN;
        RESULT : out BIT_VECTOR(1 to 6));
end test;

architecture BEHAVIOR of test is
begin
    RESULT <= add_sub(ARG1, ARG2, ADD);
end BEHAVIOR;
```

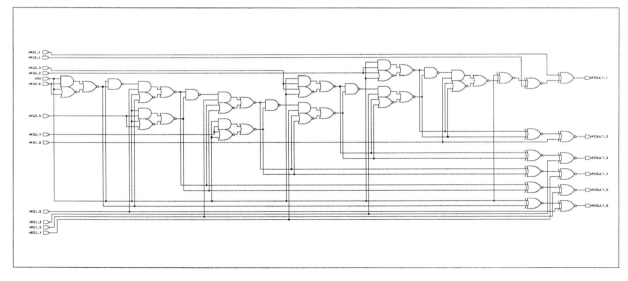

Count Zeros: Combinational Version

The count-zeros example is a design problem where an 8-bit value is given. The specifications state that the circuit is to first determine if the value is legal and then to compute the number of zeros in the string. This computation must be completed in a single clock cycle. A legal value is one that contains only one consecutive series of zeros. If more than one series of zeros appears, then the value is illegal. A value consisting entirely of 1's is defined as a legal value. If a value is illegal, then the count of zeros is set to zero. For example, the value 00000000 is legal and has 8 zeros; value 11000111 is legal and has 3 zeros; value 001111100 is not legal and therefore has no zeros.

The VHDL description implementing this problem is shown below. It consists of a single process with a for loop which iterates across each bit in the data. At each iteration, a temporary variable (TEMP_COUNT) is updated with the count of zeros encountered. Other temporary variables (SEEN_ZERO and SEEN_TRAILING) are used to keep track of when the beginning and end of the first sequence of zeros is detected.

If a zero is detected after the end of the first sequence of zeros, the count is reset to zero, and error is set to true and the loop is exited.

```vhdl
entity COUNT_COMB_VHDL is
  port(DATA: in  BIT_VECTOR(7 downto 0);
     COUNT: out INTEGER range 0 to 8;
     ERROR: out BOOLEAN);
end;

architecture BEHAVIOR of COUNT_COMB_VHDL is
begin

  process(DATA)
    variable SEEN_ZERO, SEEN_TRAILING : BOOLEAN;
    variable TEMP_COUNT : INTEGER range 0 to 8;

  begin
    ERROR <= FALSE;
    SEEN_ZERO := FALSE;
    SEEN_TRAILING := FALSE;

    TEMP_COUNT := 0;

    for I in 0 to 7 loop
      if(SEEN_TRAILING and DATA(I) = '0') then
        TEMP_COUNT := 0;
        ERROR <= TRUE;
        exit;
      elsif(SEEN_ZERO and DATA(I) = '1') then
        SEEN_TRAILING := TRUE;
      elsif(DATA(I) = '0') then
        SEEN_ZERO := TRUE;
        TEMP_COUNT := TEMP_COUNT + 1;
      end if;
    end loop;

    COUNT <= TEMP_COUNT;
  end process;

end BEHAVIOR;
```

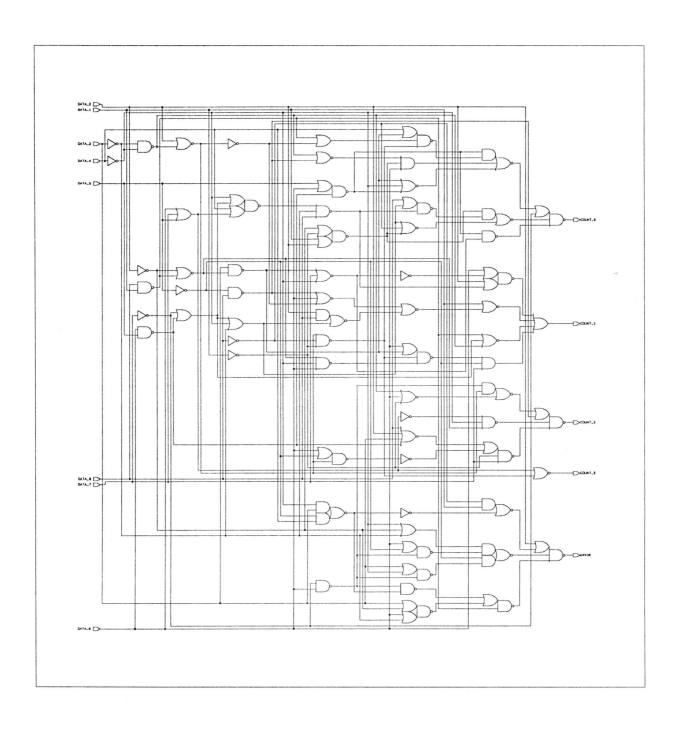

Count Zeros: Sequential Version

Assume that the specifications for the count zeros problem has changed slightly. The circuit now accepts the 8-bit string serially. Additionally, it generates a data_ready signal whenever valid data is available at the outputs. The circuit has valid outputs once it has completed processing all eight input bits or if the current bit of the input string causes the string to be illegal. To store the current state of the machine (count of zeros, count of bits processed, and current legal status), flip-flops are explicitly instantiated. The combination logic is specified in another module and connected to the flip-flops.

```
entity COUNT_SEQ_VHDL is
  port(DATA, CLK: in BIT;
     RESET, READ: in BOOLEAN;
     COUNT: buffer INTEGER range 0 to 8;
     IS_LEGAL: out BOOLEAN;
     COUNT_READY: out BOOLEAN);
end;

architecture BEHAVIOR of COUNT_SEQ_VHDL is
begin
  process
    variable SEEN_ZERO, SEEN_TRAILING : BOOLEAN;
    variable BITS_SEEN: INTEGER range 0 to 7;
  begin
    wait until CLK'event and CLK = '1';

    if(RESET) then
      COUNT_READY <= FALSE;
      IS_LEGAL <= TRUE;
      SEEN_ZERO := FALSE;
      SEEN_TRAILING := FALSE;
      COUNT <= 0;
      BITS_SEEN := 0;
    else
      if(READ) then
        if(SEEN_TRAILING and DATA = '0') then
          IS_LEGAL <= FALSE;
          COUNT <= 0;
          COUNT_READY <= TRUE;
        elsif(SEEN_ZERO and DATA = '1') then
          SEEN_TRAILING := TRUE;
        elsif(DATA = '0') then
          SEEN_ZERO := TRUE;
          COUNT <= COUNT + 1;
        end if;

        if(BITS_SEEN = 7) then
          COUNT_READY <= TRUE;
        else
          BITS_SEEN :=  BITS_SEEN + 1;
        end if;

      end if;
    end if;
  end process;
end BEHAVIOR;
```

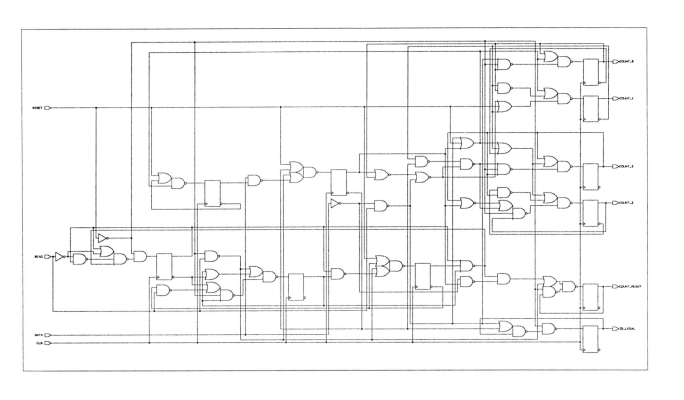

Drink Machine:
State Machine Version

The next design is a vending control unit for a drink vending machine. This circuit interfaces with a coin input unit, a change dispensing unit, and a drink dispensing unit. From the coin input unit, input signals are nickel_in (nickel deposited), dime_in (dime deposited), and quarter_in (quarter deposited). Outputs from the vending control unit are nickel_out (nickel change) and dime_out (dime change) to the change dispensing unit, and dispense (dispense drink) to the drink dispensing unit.

The price of the drink is 35 cents. The first VHDL description for this design uses a state machine description style.

```
entity DRINK_STATE_VHDL is
  port(NICKEL_IN, DIME_IN, QUARTER_IN, RESET:
      BOOLEAN;
    CLK: BIT;
    NICKEL_OUT, DIME_OUT, DISPENSE: out
        BOOLEAN);
end;

architecture BEHAVIOR of DRINK_STATE_VHDL is
  type STATE_TYPE is (IDLE, FIVE, TEN, TWENTY_FIVE,
      FIFTEEN, THIRTY, TWENTY, OWE_DIME);
  signal CURRENT_STATE, NEXT_STATE: STATE_TYPE;
begin

  process
  begin
    -- Default assignments
    NEXT_STATE <= CURRENT_STATE;
    NICKEL_OUT <= FALSE;
    DIME_OUT <= FALSE;
    DISPENSE <= FALSE;
```

```
    -- Synchronous reset
    if(RESET) then
      NEXT_STATE <= IDLE;
    else

      -- State transitions and output logic
      case CURRENT_STATE is
        when IDLE =>
          if(NICKEL_IN) then
            NEXT_STATE <= FIVE;
          elsif(DIME_IN) then
            NEXT_STATE <= TEN;
          elsif(QUARTER_IN) then
            NEXT_STATE <= TWENTY_FIVE;
          end if;

        when FIVE =>
          if(NICKEL_IN) then
            NEXT_STATE <= TEN;
          elsif(DIME_IN) then
            NEXT_STATE <= FIFTEEN;
          elsif(QUARTER_IN) then
            NEXT_STATE <= THIRTY;
          end if;

        when TEN =>
          if(NICKEL_IN) then
            NEXT_STATE <= FIFTEEN;
          elsif(DIME_IN) then
            NEXT_STATE <= TWENTY;
          elsif(QUARTER_IN) then
            NEXT_STATE <= IDLE;
            DISPENSE <= TRUE;
          end if;

        when FIFTEEN =>
          if(NICKEL_IN) then
            NEXT_STATE <= TWENTY;
          elsif(DIME_IN) then
            NEXT_STATE <= TWENTY_FIVE;
          elsif(QUARTER_IN) then
            NEXT_STATE <= IDLE;
            DISPENSE <= TRUE;
            NICKEL_OUT <= TRUE;
          end if;

        when TWENTY =>
          if(NICKEL_IN) then
```

```
    NEXT_STATE <= TWENTY_FIVE;           DISPENSE <= TRUE;
  elsif(DIME_IN) then                    NICKEL_OUT <= TRUE;
    NEXT_STATE <= THIRTY;              elsif(QUARTER_IN) then
  elsif(QUARTER_IN) then                 NEXT_STATE <= OWE_DIME;
    NEXT_STATE <= IDLE;                  DISPENSE <= TRUE;
    DISPENSE <= TRUE;                    DIME_OUT <= TRUE;
    DIME_OUT <= TRUE;                  end if;
  end if;

when TWENTY_FIVE =>                  when OWE_DIME =>
  if(NICKEL_IN) then                   NEXT_STATE <= IDLE;
    NEXT_STATE <= THIRTY;              DIME_OUT <= TRUE;
  elsif(DIME_IN) then
    NEXT_STATE <= IDLE;
    DISPENSE <= TRUE;                end case;
  elsif(QUARTER_IN) then             end if;
    NEXT_STATE <= IDLE;            end process;
    DISPENSE <= TRUE;
    DIME_OUT <= TRUE;
    NICKEL_OUT <= TRUE;           -- Synchronize state value with clock.
  end if;                         -- This causes it to be stored in flip flops
                                  process
when THIRTY =>                    begin
  if(NICKEL_IN) then               wait until CLK'event and CLK = '1';
    NEXT_STATE <= IDLE;             CURRENT_STATE <= NEXT_STATE;
    DISPENSE <= TRUE;            end process;
  elsif(DIME_IN) then
    NEXT_STATE <= IDLE;         end BEHAVIOR;
```

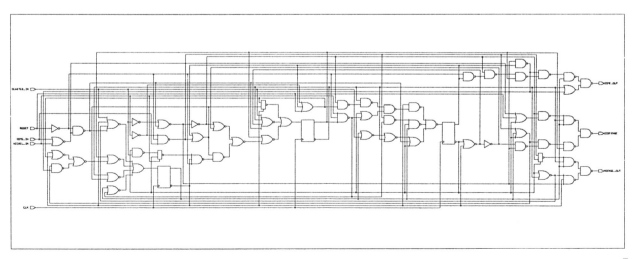

Drink Machine:
Count Nickels Version

In this version, a counter counts the number of nickels deposited.

```
entity DRINK_COUNT_VHDL is
  port(NICKEL_IN, DIME_IN, QUARTER_IN, RESET:
      BOOLEAN;
    CLK: BIT;
    NICKEL_OUT, DIME_OUT, DISPENSE: out
      BOOLEAN);
end;

architecture BEHAVIOR of DRINK_COUNT_VHDL is
  signal current_nickel_count, next_nickel_count :
INTEGER
range 0 to 7;
  signal CURRENT_RETURN_CHANGE,
      NEXT_RETURN_CHANGE : BOOLEAN;
begin

  process
    variable TEMP_NICKEL_COUNT :
        INTEGER range 0 to 12;
  begin
    -- Default assignments
    NICKEL_OUT <= FALSE;
    DIME_OUT <= FALSE;
    DISPENSE <= FALSE;
    NEXT_NICKEL_COUNT <= 0;
    NEXT_RETURN_CHANGE <= FALSE;

    -- Synchronous reset
    if(not RESET) then
      TEMP_NICKEL_COUNT :=
          CURRENT_NICKEL_COUNT;

    -- Check whether money has come in
    if (NICKEL_IN) then
      TEMP_NICKEL_COUNT :=
          TEMP_NICKEL_COUNT + 1;
    elsif(DIME_IN) then
      TEMP_NICKEL_COUNT :=
          TEMP_NICKEL_COUNT + 2;
    elsif(QUARTER_IN) then
      TEMP_NICKEL_COUNT :=
          TEMP_NICKEL_COUNT + 5;
    end if;

    -- Enough deposited so far?
    if(TEMP_NICKEL_COUNT >= 7) then
      TEMP_NICKEL_COUNT :=
          TEMP_NICKEL_COUNT - 7;
      DISPENSE <= TRUE;
    end if;

    -- Return change
    if(TEMP_NICKEL_COUNT >= 1 or
      CURRENT_RETURN_CHANGE) then
      if(TEMP_NICKEL_COUNT >= 2) then
        DIME_OUT <= TRUE;
        TEMP_NICKEL_COUNT :=
            TEMP_NICKEL_COUNT - 2;
        NEXT_RETURN_CHANGE <= TRUE;
      end if;

      if(TEMP_NICKEL_COUNT = 1) then
        NICKEL_OUT <= TRUE;
        TEMP_NICKEL_COUNT :=
            TEMP_NICKEL_COUNT - 1;
      end if;
    end if;
    NEXT_NICKEL_COUNT <=
        TEMP_NICKEL_COUNT;
  end if;
  end process;

  -- Remember the return_change flag and
  -- the nickel count for the next cycle
  process
  begin
    wait until CLK'event and CLK = '1';
    CURRENT_RETURN_CHANGE <=
        NEXT_RETURN_CHANGE;
    CURRENT_NICKEL_COUNT <=
        NEXT_NICKEL_COUNT;
  end process;

end BEHAVIOR;
```

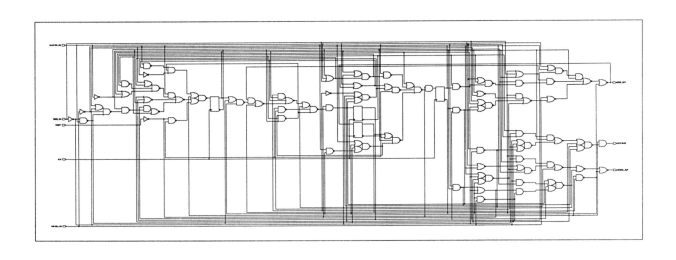

Carry Lookahead Adder

This example demonstrates the use of concurrent procedure calls to build a 32-bit carry lookahead adder. The adder is built by grouping the 32-bit input into eight slices of four bits each. Each of the eight slices computes propagate and generate values using the "PG" procedure. "propagate" is '1' for a bit position if that position will propagate a carry from the next lower position to the next higher position. "generate" is '1' for a bit position if that position will generate a carry to the next higher position regardless of the carry-in from the next lower position.

The carry lookahead logic reads inputted carry-in and the propagate and generate information computed from the inputs. It computes the carry value for each bit position. This makes the addition operation to be simply an "xor" of the inputs and the carry values.

The carry values are computed by a three level tree of four-bit carry lookahead blocks. The first-level of the tree computes the 32 carry values and eight group propagate and generate values. The first-level group propagate and generate values tell if the group of bits will propagate and generate carry values from the next lower group to the next higher. The first-level lookahead blocks read the group carry computed at the second-level. The second-level lookahead blocks read the group propagate and generate information of four first-level blocks and compute their group propagate and generate information. They also read group carry information computed at the third level to compute the carrys for each of the third-level blocks.

The third-level block reads the propagate and generate information of the second level to compute a propagate and generate value for the entire adder. It also reads the external carry to compute each second-level carry. The carry out for the adder is '1' if the third-level generate is '1', or if the third-level propagate is '1' and the external carry is '1'.

The third-level carry lookahead block is capable of processing four second-level blocks. Since there are only two, the high-order two bits of the computed carry are ignored, the high-order two bits of the generate input to the third level is set to zero, and the propagate high-order bits are set to one. This causes the unused portion to propagate carries but not to generate them.

This structure is illustrated at right:

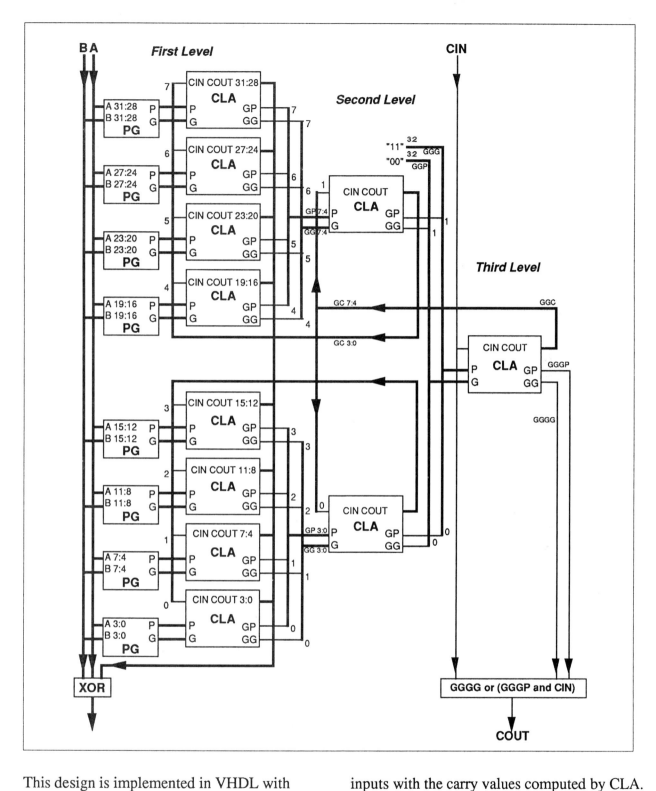

This design is implemented in VHDL with four procedures:

CLA: A four-bit carry lookahead block.

PG: Computes first-level propagate and generate information.

SUM: Computes the sum by "xor"ing the

inputs with the carry values computed by CLA.

BITSLICE: Collects the first-level CLA blocks, the PG computations, and the SUM. This procedure performs all the work for a four-bit value except the second and third-level lookahead.

This example shows the VHDL description of the adder.

```
package LOCAL is
  constant N:  INTEGER := 4;

  procedure BITSLICE(A, B: in BIT_VECTOR(3 downto 0);
            CIN: in BIT;
            signal S: out BIT_VECTOR(3 downto 0);
            signal GP, GG: out BIT);
  procedure PG(A, B: in BIT_VECTOR(3 downto 0);
            P, G: out BIT_VECTOR(3 downto 0));
  function SUM(A, B, C: in BIT_VECTOR(3 downto 0))
            return BIT_VECTOR;
  procedure CLA(P, G : in BIT_VECTOR(3 downto 0);
            CIN: in BIT;
            C : out BIT_VECTOR(3 downto 0);
            signal GP, GG: out BIT);
end LOCAL;

use WORK.LOCAL.ALL;
package body LOCAL is


-------------------------------------------------
-- compute sum and group outputs from a, b, cin
-------------------------------------------------


  procedure BITSLICE(A, B: in BIT_VECTOR(3 downto 0);
            CIN: in BIT;
            signal S: out BIT_VECTOR(3 downto 0);
            signal GP, GG: out BIT) is

  variable P, G, C: BIT_VECTOR(3 downto 0);
  begin
   PG(A, B, P, G);
   CLA(P, G, CIN, C, GP, GG);
   S <= SUM(A, B, C);
  end;


-------------------------------------------------
-- compute propagate and generate from input bits
-------------------------------------------------


  procedure PG(A, B: in BIT_VECTOR(3 downto 0);
            P, G: out BIT_VECTOR(3 downto 0)) is
```

```
begin
 P := A or B;
 G := A and B;
end;


-------------------------------------------------
-- compute sum from the input bits and the carries
-------------------------------------------------


function SUM(A, B, C: BIT_VECTOR(3 downto 0))
            return BIT_VECTOR is
begin
 return(A xor B xor C);
end;


-------------------------------------------------
-- 4-bit carry-lookahead block
-------------------------------------------------


procedure CLA(P, G : in BIT_VECTOR(3 downto 0);
        CIN: in BIT;
        C : out BIT_VECTOR(3 downto 0);
        signal GP, GG: out BIT) is

  variable TEMP_GP, TEMP_GG, LAST_C: BIT;
begin
 TEMP_GP := P(0);
 TEMP_GG := G(0);
 LAST_C := CIN;
 C(0) := CIN;

 for I in 1 to N-1 loop
   TEMP_GP := TEMP_GP and P(I);
   TEMP_GG := (TEMP_GG and P(I)) or G(I);
   LAST_C := (LAST_C and P(I-1)) or G(I-1);
   C(I) := LAST_C;
 end loop;

  GP <= TEMP_GP;
  GG <= TEMP_GG;
 end;
end LOCAL;

use WORK.LOCAL.ALL;
```

```
-- A 32 bit carry lookahead adder
```

```vhdl
entity ADDER is
  port(A, B: in BIT_VECTOR(31 downto 0); CIN: in BIT;
    S: out BIT_VECTOR(31 downto 0); COUT: out BIT);
end ADDER;

ARCHITECTURE BEHAVIOR of ADDER is

  signal GG,GP,GC: BIT_VECTOR(7 downto 0);
  -- First-level
  -- gen, prop, carry
  -- Second-level gen, prop, carry
  signal GGG, GGP, GGC: BIT_VECTOR(3 downto 0);
  signal GGGG, GGGP: BIT;
  -- Third-level gen., prop.

begin
  -- Compute Sum and first-level Generate and Propagate
  -- Use input data and the first-level Carrys computed
  -- later.
  BITSLICE(A( 3 downto  0),B( 3 downto  0),GC(0),
      S( 3 downto  0),GP(0), GG(0));
  BITSLICE(A( 7 downto  4),B( 7 downto  4),GC(1),
      S( 7 downto  4),GP(1), GG(1));
  BITSLICE(A(11 downto  8),B(11 downto  8),GC(2),
      S(11 downto  8),GP(2), GG(2));
  BITSLICE(A(15 downto 12),B(15 downto 12),GC(3),
      S(15 downto 12),GP(3), GG(3));
  BITSLICE(A(19 downto 16),B(19 downto 16),GC(4),
      S(19 downto 16),GP(4), GG(4));
  BITSLICE(A(23 downto 20),B(23 downto 20),GC(5),
      S(23 downto 20),GP(5), GG(5));
  BITSLICE(A(27 downto 24),B(27 downto 24),GC(6),
      S(27 downto 24),GP(6), GG(6));
  BITSLICE(A(31 downto 28),B(31 downto 28),GC(7),
      S(31 downto 28),GP(7), GG(7));

  -- Compute first-level Carrys and second-level generate
  -- and propagate.
  -- Use first-level Generate, Propagate, and second-level
  -- carry.
  process(GP, GG, GGC)
    variable TEMP: BIT_VECTOR(3 downto 0);
  begin
    CLA(GP(3 downto 0), GG(3 downto 0), GGC(0), TEMP,
        GGP(0), GGG(0));
```

```vhdl
    GC(3 downto 0) <= TEMP;
  end process;

  process(GP, GG, GGC)
    variable TEMP: BIT_VECTOR(3 downto 0);
  begin
    CLA (GP(7 downto 4), GG(7 downto 4), GGC(1), TEMP,
        GGP(1), GGG(1));
    GC(7 downto 4) <= TEMP;
  end process;

  -- Compute second-level Carry and third-level generate
  -- and propagate
  -- Use second-level generate, propagate and Carry-in
  -- (CIN).
  process(GGP, GGG, CIN)
    variable TEMP: BIT_VECTOR(3 downto 0);
  begin
    CLA(GGP, GGG, CIN, TEMP, GGGP, GGGG);
    GGC <= TEMP;
  end process;

  -- Assign unused bits of second-level Generate and
  -- Propagate
  GGP(3 downto 2) <= "11";
  GGG(3 downto 2) <= "00";

  -- Compute Carry-out (COUT).
  -- Use Third-level Generate and Propagate
  -- and carry-in (CIN).
  COUT <= GGGG or (GGGP and CIN);
end BEHAVIOR;
```

Implementation Details

In this implementation, procedures were used to compute the design. The procedures could have been written as separate entities and been invoked via component instantiation. This would cause a hierarchical design to be produced, since the VHDL compiler does not collapse the hierarchy of entities, while it does collapse the procedure call hierarchy into one design. Note that the keyword "signal" is included before some of the interface parameter declarations. This is required for "out" formal parameters where the actual parameters are signals.

The "C" out parameter of the "CLA" procedure was not declared as a signal. This makes illegal use it in a concurrent procedure call (since only signals may be used in such calls). To overcome this, a procedure was created with a temporary variable "TEMP". This variable receives the value of the "C" parameter and then assigns it to the appropriate signal. This generally is a useful technique.

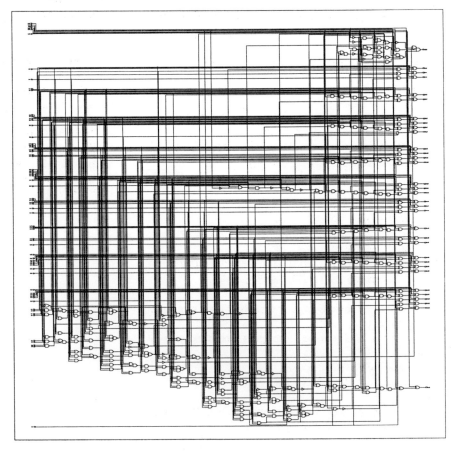

Serial To Parallel Converter: Counter

This example shows the design of a serial to parallel converter. It reads a serial input and produces an 8-bit output. The design has the following inputs:

SERIAL_IN — Serial input data

RESET — When set to '1', will cause the converter to reset. All outputs are set to zero, and the converter is made ready to read the next serial word.

CLOCK — The value of the RESET and SERIAL_IN is read on the positive transition of this clock. Outputs of the converter are valid only on positive transitions also.

The design produces the following outputs:

PARALLEL_OUT — Eight bit value read from the SERIAL_IN port.

READ_ENABLE — When this output is '1' on the positive transition of CLOCK, then the data on PARALLEL_OUT is available for reading.

PARITY_ERROR — When this output is '1' on the positive transition of CLOCK, then a parity error was detected on the SERIAL_IN port. Once a parity error has been detected, the converter freezes until restarted by the RESET port.

Input Format

When no data is being transmitted to the serial port, it should be kept at a value of '0'. Each eight bit value requires ten clock cycles to read. In the first cycle, a '1' is placed on the serial input. This indicates that an eight bit value follows. The next eight cycles are used to transmit the eight bit value. The most significant bit is transmitted first. The tenth and final cycle is used to transmit the parity of the eight bit value. It must be '0' if there were an even number of '1's in the 8-bit data, and '1' otherwise. If the converter detects a parity error, then the PARITY_ERROR output is set to '1' and it waits until it is reset.

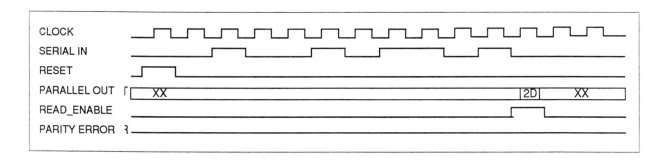

On the eleventh cycle, the READ_ENABLE output is changed to '1', and the 8-bit value may be read from the PARALLEL_OUT port. If the SERIAL_IN port is a '1' on the eleventh cycle, then another eight bit value is read immediately, otherwise the converter waits for it to go to '1'.

Implementation Details

The converter is implemented with a four-state finite state machine with synchronous reset. When a reset is detected, the WAIT_FOR_START state is entered. The following describes each state:

WAIT_FOR_START — Stay in this state until a '1' is detected on the serial input. When a '1' is detected, clear the parallel_out registers and go to the READ_BITS state.

READ_BITS — If the current_bit_position counter is 8, then all eight bits were read. Check the parity and go to the ALLOW_READ state if OK, otherwise go to the PARITY_ERROR state. If all eight bits have not yet been read, then the set the appropriate bit in the parallel_out buffer to the serial_in, compute the parity of the bits read so far, and increment the current_bit_position.

ALLOW_READ — This is the state where the outside world reads the parallel_out value. It immediately goes back to the WAIT_FOR_START state.

PARITY_ERROR_DETECTED — When in this state, the parity_error output is set to '1', and nothing else is done.

This design has four values stored in registers:

CURRENT_STATE — Remembers the state as of the last clock edge.

CURRENT_BIT_POSITION — Remembers how many bits have been read so far.

CURRENT_PARITY — Keeps a running "xor" of the bits read.

CURRENT_PARALLEL_OUT — Stores each parallel bit as it is found.

The design is broken into two processes: NEXT_ST which is combinational and performs all the computations. SYNCH which is sequential and causes the registering of the stored values discussed above. Each registered signal is broken into two signals, CURRENT_... and NEXT_... The NEXT_... signals hold values computed by the NEXT_ST process. The CURRENT_... signals hold the values driven by the SYNCH process. The CURRENT_... signals keep the values of the NEXT_... signals as of the last clock edge.

The NEXT_ST process starts by first assigning default values to all signals it drives. This means that later in the process, a signal assignment is created only when a value should be driven onto a signal which is not the default. It also guarantees that all signals are driven under all conditions. Next, the RESET input is processed. If RESET is not active, then a "case" statement determines the current state. Each "when" clause performs the work appropriate. State transitions are performed by assigning to the NEXT_STATE signal.

The serial to parallel conversion is performed by the lines:

```
NEXT_PARALLEL_OUT(CURRENT_BIT_POSITION)<=
    SERIAL_IN
NEXT_BIT_POSITION <=
    CURRENT_BIT_POSITION + 1;
```

The first assigns a particular bit of the parallel output, the second increments the next bit position that will be assigned.

```
-- serial to parallel converter
-- This package declares types used in the reset of the
-- design.
package TYPES is
  type STATE_TYPE is (WAIT_FOR_START, READ_BITS,
        PARITY_ERROR_DETECTED, ALLOW_READ);
  constant PARALLEL_BIT_COUNT: INTEGER := 8;
  subtype PARALLEL_RANGE is INTEGER range 0 to
        (PARALLEL_BIT_COUNT-1);
  subtype PARALLEL_TYPE is
        BIT_VECTOR(PARALLEL_RANGE);
end TYPES;
```

```
use WORK.TYPES.ALL;
-- Use the TYPES package

entity SER_PAR is
-- Declare the interface
  port(SERIAL_IN, CLOCK, RESET: in BIT;
      PARALLEL_OUT: out PARALLEL_TYPE;
      PARITY_ERROR, READ_ENABLE: out BIT);
end;

architecture BEHAVIOR of SER_PAR is
-- Signals for stored values
  signal CURRENT_STATE, NEXT_STATE: STATE_TYPE;

  signal CURRENT_PARITY, NEXT_PARITY: BIT;
  signal CURRENT_BIT_POSITION,
      NEXT_BIT_POSITION:
        INTEGER range PARALLEL_BIT_COUNT
            downto 0;
  signal CURRENT_PARALLEL_OUT,
      NEXT_PARALLEL_OUT: PARALLEL_TYPE;
begin

--
-- This process computes all outputs, the next state and
-- the next value of all stored values.
--
NEXT_ST: process(SERIAL_IN, CURRENT_STATE,
            RESET,
            CURRENT_BIT_POSITION,CURRENT_PARITY,
            CURRENT_PARALLEL_OUT)
  begin
    PARITY_ERROR <= '0';
-- Default values for all
    READ_ENABLE <= '0';
  -- outputs and stored values
    NEXT_STATE <= CURRENT_STATE;
    NEXT_BIT_POSITION <= 0;
    NEXT_PARITY <= '0';
    NEXT_PARALLEL_OUT <=
        CURRENT_PARALLEL_OUT;
    if(RESET = '1') then
-- Synchronous reset
      NEXT_STATE <= WAIT_FOR_START;
    else
      case CURRENT_STATE is
```

```
-- State dependent processing
    when WAIT_FOR_START =>
     if(SERIAL_IN = '1') then
      NEXT_STATE <= READ_BITS;
      NEXT_PARALLEL_OUT<=
      PARALLEL_TYPE'(others=>'0');
     end if;
    when READ_BITS =>
     if(CURRENT_BIT_POSITION =
          PARALLEL_BIT_COUNT) then
      if(CURRENT_PARITY = SERIAL_IN) then
       NEXT_STATE <= ALLOW_READ;
       READ_ENABLE <= '1';
      else
       NEXT_STATE <= PARITY_ERROR_DETECTED;
      end if;
     else
     NEXT_PARALLEL_OUT(CURRENT_BIT_POSITION)
        <=SERIAL_IN;
     NEXT_BIT_POSITION <=
        CURRENT_BIT_POSITION + 1;
     NEXT_PARITY <= CURRENT_PARITY xor
        SERIAL_IN;
     end if;

    when PARITY_ERROR_DETECTED =>
     PARITY_ERROR <= '1';
    when ALLOW_READ =>
     NEXT_STATE <= WAIT_FOR_START;
   end case;
  end if;
 end process;
--
-- This process remembers the stored values across
-- clock cycles
--
 SYNCH: process
 begin
  wait until CLOCK'event and CLOCK = '1';
  CURRENT_STATE <= NEXT_STATE;
  CURRENT_BIT_POSITION <= NEXT_BIT_POSITION;
  CURRENT_PARITY <= NEXT_PARITY;
  CURRENT_PARALLEL_OUT <= NEXT_PARALLEL_OUT;
 end process;

 PARALLEL_OUT <= CURRENT_PARALLEL_OUT;
end BEHAVIOR;
```

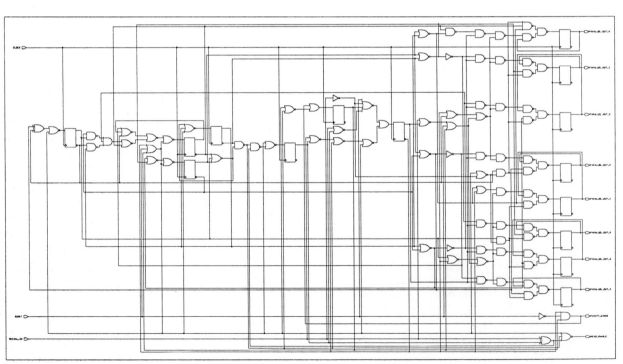

Serial To Parallel Converter - Shifter

This section describes a second implementation of the serial to parallel converter which performs the same function as the previous one, but uses a different algorithm to do the conversion. In the previous implementation, a counter was kept to indicate which bit of the output to set each time a new serial bit was read. In this implementation, the serial bits are shifted into place. Before the conversion takes place, a '1' is placed in the least-significant bit position. When that one is shifted beyond the most significant position (position 0) the signal NEXT_HIGH_BIT is set to one and the conversion is complete.

The listing of the second implementation follows. The differences are highlighted in bold. All the differences center around the removal of the ..._BIT_POSITION signal, addition of ..._HIGH_BIT signal, and the change in the way NEXT_PARALLEL_OUT is computed.

```vhdl
-- serial to parallel converter
-- This package declares types used in the reset of the
-- design.
package TYPES is
  type STATE_TYPE is (WAIT_FOR_START, READ_BITS,
          PARITY_ERROR_DETECTED, ALLOW_READ);
  constant PARALLEL_BIT_COUNT: INTEGER := 8;
  subtype PARALLEL_RANGE is INTEGER range 0 to
    (PARALLEL_BIT_COUNT-1);
  subtype PARALLEL_TYPE is
    BIT_VECTOR(PARALLEL_RANGE);
end TYPES;

use WORK.TYPES.ALL;
-- Use the TYPES package

entity SER_PAR is
-- Declare the interface
  port(SERIAL_IN, CLOCK, RESET: in BIT;
      PARALLEL_OUT: out PARALLEL_TYPE;
      PARITY_ERROR, READ_ENABLE: out BIT);
end;

architecture BEHAVIOR of SER_PAR is
-- Signals for stored values
  signal CURRENT_STATE, NEXT_STATE: STATE_TYPE;

  signal CURRENT_PARITY, NEXT_PARITY: BIT;
  signal CURRENT_HIGH_BIT, NEXT_HIGH_BIT: BIT;
  signal CURRENT_PARALLEL_OUT,
NEXT_PARALLEL_OUT:
PARALLEL_TYPE;
begin

--
-- This process computes all outputs, the next state and
-- the next value of all stored values.
--
NEXT_ST: process(SERIAL_IN, CURRENT_STATE,
        RESET, CURRENT_HIGH_BIT,
              CURRENT_PARITY,
              CURRENT_PARALLEL_OUT)
  begin
    PARITY_ERROR <= '0';
-- Default values for all
    READ_ENABLE <= '0';
-- outputs and stored values
    NEXT_STATE <= CURRENT_STATE;
```

```
      NEXT_HIGH_BIT <= '0';                       --
      NEXT_PARITY <= '0';                         -- This process remembers the stored values across
      NEXT_PARALLEL_OUT<=                         -- clock cycles
            PARALLEL_TYPE'(others=>'0');          --
                                                   SYNCH: process
      if(RESET = '1') then                         begin
-- Synchronous reset                                 wait until CLOCK'event and CLOCK = '1';
        NEXT_STATE <= WAIT_FOR_START;              CURRENT_STATE <= NEXT_STATE;
      else                                         CURRENT_HIGH_BIT <= NEXT_HIGH_BIT;
        case CURRENT_STATE is                      CURRENT_PARITY <= NEXT_PARITY;
-- State dependent processing                      CURRENT_PARALLEL_OUT <= NEXT_PARALLEL_OUT;
          when WAIT_FOR_START =>                  end process;
            if(SERIAL_IN = '1') then               PARALLEL_OUT <= CURRENT_PARALLEL_OUT;
              NEXT_STATE <= READ_BITS;           end BEHAVIOR;
        NEXT_PARALLEL_OUT<=PARALLEL_TYPE'(others=>'0');
            end if;
          when READ_BITS =>
            if(CURRENT_HIGH_BIT = '1') then
             if(CURRENT_PARITY = SERIAL_IN) then
              NEXT_STATE <= ALLOW_READ;
              READ_ENABLE <= '1';
             else
              NEXT_STATE <= PARITY_ERROR_DETECTED;
             end if;
            else
              NEXT_HIGH_BIT<=
               CURRENT_PARALLEL_OUT(0);
              NEXT_PARALLEL_OUT <=
               CURRENT_PARALLEL_OUT(1 to
                    PARALLEL_BIT_COUNT-1) & SERIAL_IN;
              NEXT_PARITY <= CURRENT_PARITY xor
                    SERIAL_IN;
            end if;
          when PARITY_ERROR_DETECTED =>
            PARITY_ERROR <= '1';
          when ALLOW_READ =>
            NEXT_STATE <= WAIT_FOR_START;
        end case;
      end if;
    end process;
```

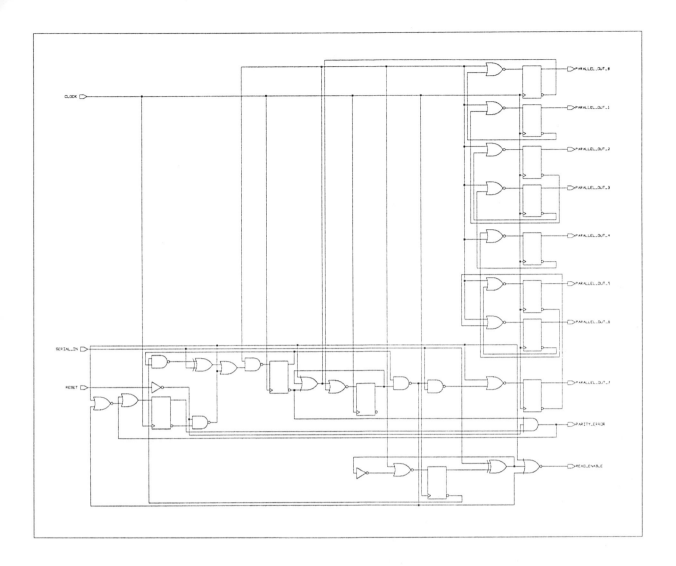

Notice that the synthesized schematic for the shifter implementation is much simpler than the first. This is because the "shifter" algorithm is inherently easier to implement in logic.

With the "count" algorithm, each of the flip-flops holding the PARALLEL_OUT bits needed logic which decoded the value stored in the BIT_POSITION flip-flops to see when to route in the value of SERIAL_IN. Additionally, the BIT_POSITION flip-flops needed an incrementer to compute their next value. In contrast, the "shifter" algorithm requires no incrementer, and no flip flops to hold BIT_POSITION. Additionally, the logic in front of most PARALLEL_OUT bits needs only to read the value of the previous flip-flop or '0' depending on whether bits are currently being read. In the "shifter" algorithm, the SERIAL_IN port needs only to be connected to the least significant bit (number 7) of the PARALLEL_OUT flip flops.

These two implementations illustrate the importance of designing efficient algorithms. Both will work properly, but the better algorithm produced a faster, more area-efficient design.

PLA

This example shows a way to build PLAs in VHDL. A function, called PLA, is written which takes in an input vector and a constant PLA table and returns the output values as specified in the PLA.

The PLA table is built as an array of "PLA_ROW". Each row is an array of "PLA_ELEMENT". Each element is either a '1', '0', '-' or ' '. The table is split into an input plane and an output plane. These are separated by a ' '. Whenever a row in the table matches the input vector, the '1's in the output plane are assigned to the output vector. A "match" is determined as follows: If there is a '0' in the table, then the input vector must have the value '0' in the corresponding position for a match. If there is a '1' in the table, then the input vector must equal a '1' in the corresponding position. If there is a '-' in the table, then that position matches anything.

Note that the PLA function does not explicitly depend on the size of the PLA. To change the PLA, you would need only to change the initialization of the TABLE constant and the initialization of the constants INPUT_COUNT, OUTPUT_COUNT and ROW_COUNT. Notice in listing that these constants were initialized to a PLA which is equivalent to the ROM shown previously. Accordingly, the synthesized schematic is the same as that of the ROM. This example was included mainly to illustrate the capabilities of VHDL. It would much more efficient to use a PLA input format directly; the advantage is that the model is an executable specification.

```
package LOCAL is
  constant INPUT_COUNT: INTEGER := 3;
  constant OUTPUT_COUNT: INTEGER := 5;
  constant ROW_COUNT: INTEGER := 6;
  constant ROW_SIZE: INTEGER := INPUT_COUNT +
                    OUTPUT_COUNT + 1;
  type PLA_ELEMENT is ('1', '0', '-', ' ');
  type PLA_VECTOR is
        array (INTEGER range <>) of PLA_ELEMENT;
  subtype PLA_ROW is
        PLA_VECTOR (ROW_SIZE - 1 downto 0);
  subtype PLA_OUTPUT is
        PLA_VECTOR(OUTPUT_COUNT - 1 downto 0);
  type PLA_TABLE is
        array(ROW_COUNT - 1 downto 0) of PLA_ROW;

  function PLA(IN_VECTOR: BIT_VECTOR;
        TABLE: PLA_TABLE)
      return BIT_VECTOR;
end LOCAL;

package body LOCAL is
  use WORK.LOCAL.all;

  function PLA(IN_VECTOR: BIT_VECTOR; TABLE:
PLA_TABLE)
        return BIT_VECTOR is
    subtype RESULT_TYPE is
          BIT_VECTOR(OUTPUT_COUNT - 1 downto 0);
    variable RESULT: RESULT_TYPE;
    variable ROW: PLA_ROW;
    variable MATCH: BOOLEAN;
    variable IN_POS: INTEGER;
  begin
    RESULT := RESULT_TYPE'(others => BIT'( '0' ));

    for I in TABLE'range loop
      ROW := TABLE(I);
```

```
MATCH := TRUE;                                              return(RESULT);
IN_POS := IN_VECTOR'left;                                 end;
                                                        end LOCAL;
-- and plane
for J in ROW_SIZE - 1 downto                            use WORK.LOCAL.all;
        OUTPUT_COUNT loop
  if(ROW(J) = PLA_ELEMENT'( '1' )) then  MATCH :=        entity PLA_VHDL is
   MATCH and                                              port(IN_VECTOR: BIT_VECTOR(2 downto 0);
        (IN_VECTOR(IN_POS) = BIT'( '1' ));                  OUT_VECTOR: out BIT_VECTOR(4 downto 0));
  elsif(ROW(J) = PLA_ELEMENT'( '0' )) then              end;
   MATCH := MATCH and
        (IN_VECTOR(IN_POS) = BIT'( '0' ));              architecture BEHAVIOR of PLA_VHDL is
  end if;                                                 constant TABLE : PLA_TABLE :=
  IN_POS := IN_POS - 1;                                           PLA_TABLE'(PLA_ROW'("— 10000"),
end loop;                                                         PLA_ROW'("-1- 01000"),
                                                                  PLA_ROW'("0-0 00101"),
-- or plane                                                       PLA_ROW'("-1- 00101"),
if(MATCH) then                                                    PLA_ROW'("1-1 00101"),
  for J in RESULT'range loop                                      PLA_ROW'("-1- 00010"));
   if(ROW(J) = PLA_ELEMENT'( '1' )) then
    RESULT(J) := BIT'( '1' );
   end if;
  end loop;                                             begin
 end if;                                                 OUT_VECTOR <= PLA(IN_VECTOR, TABLE);
end loop;                                               end BEHAVIOR;
```

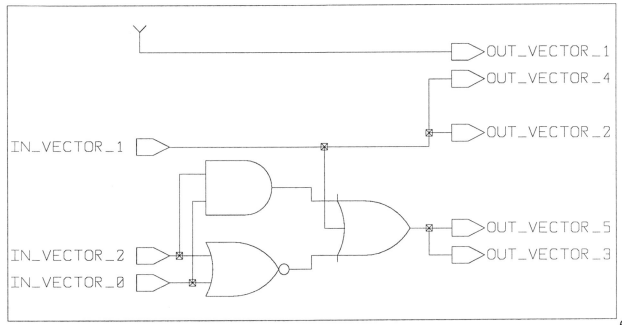

5

Clock and Timing Methods

A **pure** functional description in an HDL represents the what and the how of a design; what is missing is the when. Fundamental to system operation are the clock and timing elements of a design; they orchestrate the functional component interaction in the system. This chapter focuses on specific timing-related issues in HDL system design.

Process Independent Design

Implicit versus Explicit Timing

Explicit Timing

Implicit State

Partially Asynchronous Operation

Asynchronous Operation

Process Independent Design

One of the key benefits of an HDL based methodology is the opportunity to design in a technology independent manner. This means a deferral of the actual silicon technology choice, and an inherently more retargetable design description. Because most new large system designs contain a significant portion of previously designed logic, having "portable" designs is extremely valuable. This section introduces some of the considerations in writing process independent designs.

Clock rate and signal delay are highly process dependent system performance parameters. Placing clock rate and signal delay timing information into technology independent models is self defeating. Embedding such information in the models, even if it is considered a design goal or constraint (rather than actual performance), ties the model to a particular generation of technology. While performance goals are an important ingredient to quality of results in the synthesis process, they are better represented in a contained context (such as VHDL package constants or separate constraint files) aimed at a particular process library. The inclusion of "accurate" timing in high level models also poses a problem because the structure of the HDL code may not bear any resemblance to the physical path structures in the gate-level implementation.

An alternative to explicit inclusion of technology dependent timing in high level models is the use of a metric-free timing representation more commensurate with the level of abstraction being used for the representation of function. For an RTL description, the natural abstraction is to that of a system clock used for global synchronization; i.e., the use of an event oriented synchronization rather than time unit specification is more appropriate in the RTL domain. The abstraction process allows the deferral of the binding of physical units. The hazard of this abstraction is the isolation from physical reality. The use of synthesis directly compensates for the shortcomings of abstraction by allowing a fast path down into the targeted technologies; the technology specific representations provide the model for accurate analysis.

Asynchronous designs, by their very nature, require more specification than their synchronous counterparts. While synchronous designs can rely on a global event oriented synchronization process, asynchronous designs rely upon specific timing relationships for proper network function. This means that in order to create an accurate portrayal of circuit function all such relative relationships must be specified. The last section in this chapter addresses the issues in asynchronous HDL-based design.

Another important consideration in the preparation of technology-independent HDL models is the use of electrically based architectural decisions. Probably the most common example of an electrically based architectural decision is the choice of a bus structure. Three-state buses work great within the MOS technology families because of the utility of pass transistor networks, but in ECL, multiplexer structures are the implementation of choice. I/O pads are another portion of the design where the decisions made are primarily concerned with electrical rather than functional aspects of the network. When creating "portable" HDL models, it is important to isolate those parts of the design where technology-dependent information affects the functional description. Design hierarchy is an excellent way to achieve the isolation. Recognizing and isolating those portions of the design is an important step in technology-independent HDL model composition.

The silicon vendors offer a number of tools to speed their customers through the design process into production. One of the more successful tool offerings from the silicon vendors, in terms of designer productivity, has been the technology dependent "module compiler." Typical tools produce the layout information for RAMs , ROMs and even more complex elements such as multipliers.

The most successful of these tools are tied tightly to the particular process technology, allowing maximal use of the idiosynchrocies of the technology. The important point to note about these "module compilers" is that they exist and that they can be very useful tools.

So how do module compilers fit into technology-independent models? The answer, unfortunately, is vendor dependent. The straightforward approach is the use of structural hierarchy to insert the compiled blocks into the HDL model; these blocks are then treated as black boxes during the synthesis process, but then linked to the resultant technology-dependent design description via structural instantiation. That part is common to all environments. Some environments may provide detailed information about the module timing and interface parameters (e.g., load and drive) that will allow the synthesis tools to customize the interface logic around the "compiled modules." The simulation, however, of the complete HDL model may not be possible unless the silicon vendor provides HDL models for the compiled blocks as a matter of course. The inclusion of technology-specific compiled blocks is a matter of practical tradeoffs, but the decisions made in modeling should be explicit with respect to technology-independent modeling. A conservative approach is to use the standard part paradigm. Under this approach only commonly available modules are used (e.g., standard word width and size parameters for a RAM), while specialized configurations (e.g., 7-bit, 6K, 3 port RAM with three-state outputs) are foregone as the price for technology independence.

Hierarchy of Abstraction

Physical implementation
(no abstraction)
Transistor level models
Logic gate netlist
RTL combined structural and
functional
Algorithmic description
(highest abstraction)

Fig. 1

Parallel Hierarchy of Abstraction

Physical implementation	Measured values
Transistor level models	Continuous time
Logic gate netlist	Discrete time
RTL structural and functional	Global event synchronization
Algorithmic description	Self synchronizing

Fig. 2

Implicit Versus Explicit Timing

As synthesis technology pushes up the abstraction ladder from the explicitly defined register world of RTL design into the behavioral realm, system clocking schemes can be represented implicitly. Creeping into higher levels of abstraction opens up a new set of timing related considerations.

Two of the most useful strategies for containing the increasing complexity of digital designs are the use of abstraction and structured design. In functional design a familiar hierarchy of abstraction has evolved (fig. 1).

The progression of functional abstraction shown above leads to a parallel (and interwoven) hierarchy of abstraction for time (fig. 2).

Once a physical implementation has been realized, time is measured, not modeled. In the transistor level domain, continuous time differential equations are used to predict the time domain response of the network. At the logic level, time is still given physical units, but has been broken into discrete intervals whose granularity is determined by the technology of the network being modeled. At the RTL level time is broken out of the physical domain and into an event oriented measure, a global event. Into the algorithmic realm, totally devoid of implementation detail, time is not measured, but the concept is used for ordering algorithmic processes.

There are two break points surrounding RTL timing abstraction. Between logic and RTL time measure is changed from a physical metric to an event synchronization function. Between RTL and algorithmic descriptions the synchronization function changes from a centralized mechanism to a distributed mechanism used at the algorithmic level. As you can see, RTL timing abstraction sits precariously on the boundary of the explicit and implicit timing representation. Because timing is such a critical element to digital design, either the transformation from implicit to explicit timing must be well understood, or adequate control mechanisms must be placed into the synthesis capabilities to ensure predictable high quality results.

Explicit Timing

System timing specifications are executed using a clock system. The clock system has two main functions, clock generation and clock distribution. A well planned clock system is a prerequisite to reliable digital system operation. System clocks are usually generated from the sinusoidal output of a voltage controlled oscillator (VCO), a crystal oscillator (XO), or a voltage controlled crystal oscillator. The sinusoid is then clamped and/or divided to produce the rectangular system clock. The electronics for these generators is generally packaged into a single hybrid IC. Because of the precise electrical control required, and the general availability of pre-packaged clock generation ICs, clock generators are not considered a synthesizable portion of the design.

Clock distribution networks deliver the clock signal to the storage elements in the design. The criticality of the distribution network is determined, to a large extent, by the clocking scheme chosen. ASIC vendors provide a special set of cells and wiring schemes to deal with the problem of getting the system clock signals on the chip and then distributed to the individual clocked elements. Often large wire trunks are used in conjunction with local buffering to minimize the difference in arrival times of the clock signal at each storage element (this is also called skew

Fixed Configuration Scheme

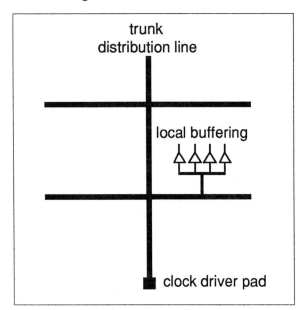

trunk
distribution line

local buffering

clock driver pad

Single-Phase Clock Waveform

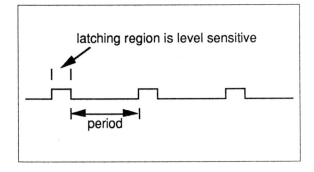

latching region is level sensitive

period

Single-Phase State Machine

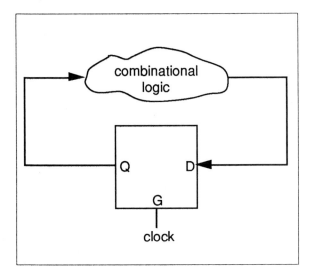

combinational
logic

Q   D

G

clock

minimization). A conceptual drawing of a fixed configuration scheme is shown above.

The disadvantage of these fixed distribution networks is that they consume a significant portion of the available silicon, and for maximal control, sophisticated interaction between the layout, timing analysis and buffering optimization tools is required.

A system clocking scheme is single-phase, multi-phase (usually two-phase), or edge-triggered. Single-phase, latch-based design requires precise control over both minimum and maximum arrival times. The attractiveness of single-phase design comes from the ability to use minimal area and delay storage elements, and the ability to "cheat" the system by designing long paths that actually cross the phase boundaries, intentionally. The latching function under this clock scheme is level sensitive, rather than edge triggered. The figures above depict a single-

phase clock waveform, and a diagrammatic view of a single phase state machine.

The most notable single phase latch machines are the Amdahl 580 and the Cray 1, which at their introduction dates, were known as complex designs that yielded high performance results. The major problem with this design style is the small tolerance to variation in device parameters to achieve a functioning machine. Local drift in either the fast or slow direction in device operation cause malfunctions that are not typically correctable by altering the external

Two-Phase Clock Waveform

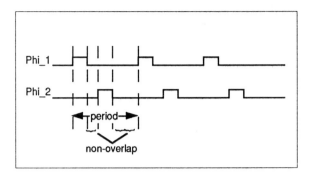

Two-Phase State Machine

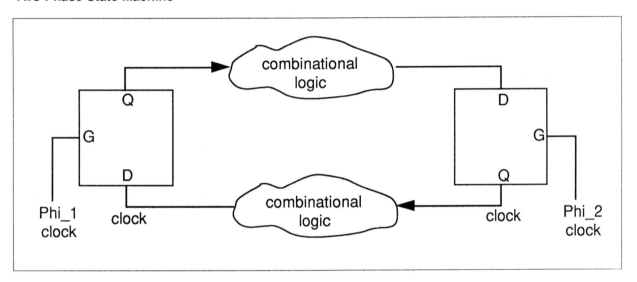

clock. This manufacturability problem is only acceptable in low volume high price applications.

The most widely used clock scheme is multi-phase. Multi-phase schemes overcome the parameter variation tolerance problem of the single-phase scheme by using a dead (non-overlap) period between active clock phases. This technique of design creates devices that can always be made to work by adjustments to the system clocks. This methodology has successfully been integrated into both high volume and

high performance design applications. The waveforms for a two-phase system and a diagram of a two-phase state machine are shown above.

The systems that have adopted a two-phase clock scheme include, the Intel 80x86 series, Bellmac 32A, Motorola MC68000 family, HP 9000, Univac 100/90 and the IBM 3090.

Multi-phase schemes are generalized from the two-phase scheme presented above. Multi-phase schemes are usually employed when the system design is expected to have

Multi-Phase Clock Waveform

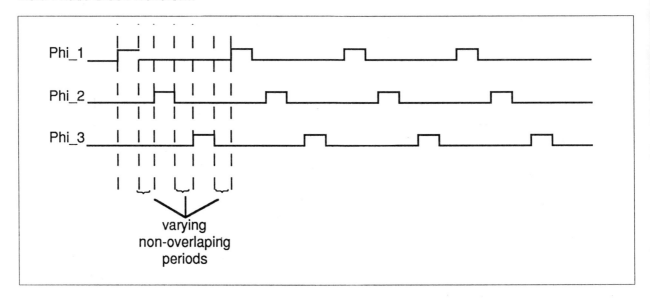

varying
non-overlaping
periods

Multi-Phase State Machine

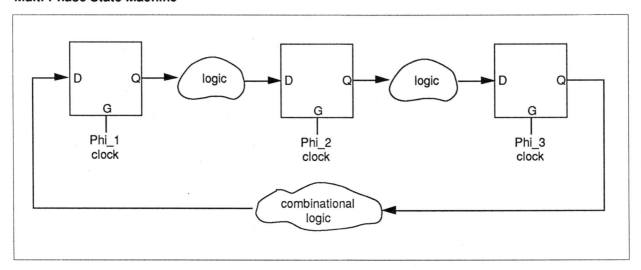

many paths of differing lengths that need to be folded into a synchronous data or control path. The two most common multi-phase schemes are the adjacent phase and skip phase methods. The skip phase method is usually constructed by cascading two or more two phase machines together, while the adjacent scheme is used to take advantage of varying non-overlap periods. The waveform and state machine diagram for the adjacent schemes are shown above.

Edge triggered design is perhaps the simplest of the clocking schemes. This methodology calls for a single system clock which feeds storage elements that are sensitive only the rising or falling edge of the clock signal, rather than its level. The waveform and state machine for this scheme are shown above.

Edge-Triggered Clock Waveform

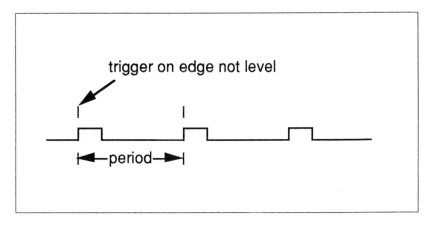

Edge-Triggered State Machine

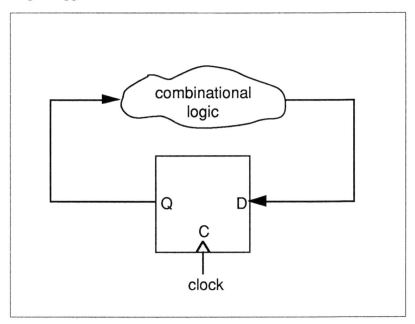

The biggest problem with edge triggered designs is their sensitivity to clock skew. Just as with single phase latch system, local timing variations can create networks that will not function properly at any clock speed. The clock distribution part of the clock system is increasingly difficult to design with the increasing complexity of ASIC devices. This fact is driving designers to apply multi-phase schemes that are not sensitive to clock skew.

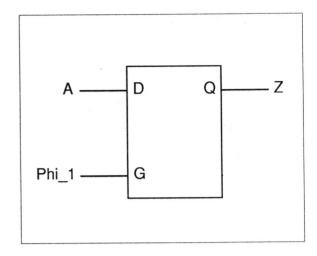

Implicit State

RTL design has typically been thought of as a paradigm where all storage elements in the network are explicitly defined. A slight push upward in the abstraction ladder allows the use of implicitly defined storage elements in the design description. Looking back at the finite state machine of Chapter 3, we see that there is no explicit definition of a register. Instead, a port signal is assigned inside of a global synchronization (wait for clock edge). This assignment encapsulated in a synchronization construct is an explicit method of implicitly identifying a register.

There are also methods to perform completely implicit storage element definition in an HDL description. The most straightforward method to describe is the incompletely specified conditional assignment. In this method, a signal is assigned a new value only under the true evaluation of some conditional expression; otherwise, the signal is not assigned to at all. In the latter case where the signal is not assigned, it should maintain its old value. This implies the creation of states. As an example, the VHDL code below and corresponding schematic show how an incompletely specified conditional assignment implicitly requires the inclusion of a latch.

```
entity LATCH_VHDL is
  port(PHI_1, A: in BIT;
       Z: out BIT);
end LATCH_VHDL;

architecture D_LATCH of LATCH_VHDL is
begin
  process(PHI_1,A)
  begin
    if(PHI_1 = '1') then
      Z <= A;
    end if;
  end process;
end D_LATCH;
```

The capability to implicitly define the storage elements of your design removes you from one level of detail and ensures technology independent storage element description. The hazard is that unnecessary states will be generated because of careless coding practices. Anytime a functional description contains a incompletely specified conditional assignment, state will be generated.

As an illustration of the utility of the implicit state definition, below we show a simple two-phase clock scheme latch design. The clock signals PHI_1 and PHI_2 are externally generated and assumed to be non-overlapping signals. The machine performs a logic function on the incoming signal, and the output is fed by the PHI_2 clocked latch. Although a somewhat trivial example, this illustrates a template for design of a two-phase system.

```
entity TWO_PHASE is
  port(PHI_1, PHI_2, A: in BIT;   Z: out BIT);
end TWO_PHASE;


architecture DUAL_PHASE of TWO_PHASE is
  signal TEMP, LOOP_BACK: BIT;
begin
  process(PHI_1,PHI_2,A,TEMP,LOOP_BACK)
  begin
```

```
if(PHI_1 = '1') then
  TEMP <= A and LOOP_BACK;
end if;

if(PHI_2 = '1') then
  LOOP_BACK <= not TEMP;
end if;

Z <= LOOP_BACK;
end process;
end;
```

The PHI_1 and PHI_2 processes contain all of their logic in this example. It is often convenient to set up input and output vectors to the PHI_1 and PHI_2 processes and then separate the logic and storage functions of the design. That is not a mandatory part of the methodology, but can often lead to a "cleaner" model.

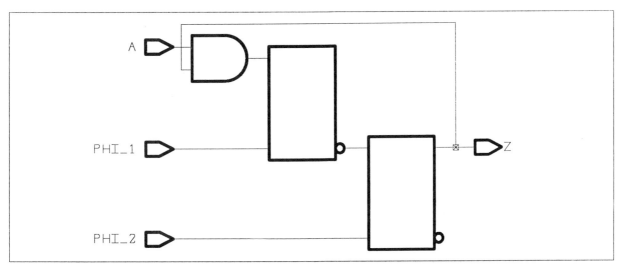

Partially Asynchronous Operation

Often in the design of synchronous systems, partial asynchronous operation is a convenient or required part of the specification. Typical, trivial, examples are system wide reset on power-up or partial system state reset on error or failure. This section introduces a straightforward style for the description of partially asynchronous networks.

It is simple to turn the Mealy state machine of Chapter 4 into a partially asynchronous machine. In this case we wish to add a new port, RESET, to put the state machine back into state S0 when the signal is high. The only portion of the state machine architecture that needs to be modified is the sequential process SYNCH. The new process description and complete schematic are shown here.

```
-- Process to hold synchronous elements (flip-flops)
SYNCH: process
begin
  -- asynchronous condition to go back to S0
```

```
if (RESET = '1') then
  CURRENT_STATE <= S0;
-- else normal synchronous operation
elsif (CLOCK'event and CLOCK = '1') then
  CURRENT_STATE <= NEXT_STATE;
end if;
end process;
```

The use of partially asynchronous operation is almost essential in all digital designs, which makes such descriptive capability a mandatory part of an HDL-based synthesis policy. The additional descriptive capability, however, can be a source of problems if used indiscriminately. For instance, it now becomes possible to describe networks with highly complex race conditions; the asynchronous part of the sequential assignments can be chained via the communicating signals between two processes resulting in interdependent asynchronous operation. It is much safer to handle the communication between two processes via synchronized signals.

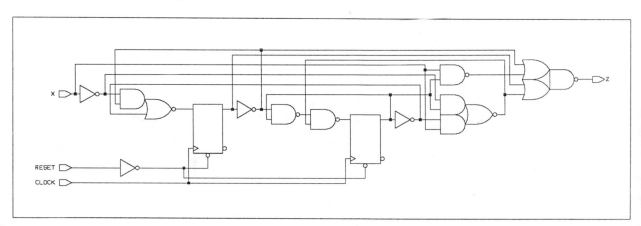

Asynchronous Operation

Most high performance systems today contain at least one subsystem that operates asynchronously. Although this design style can often complicate many issues in the design process, the benefit typically cited is an overall increase in system speed. This section introduces some of the basic considerations in HDL based asynchronous design.

The execution of operations in asynchronous machines is controlled via completion and initiation signals. The machines are designed such that the completion of one operation initiates the execution of the next consecutive operation (which is determined by the present state and/or input values).

A universal asynchronous receiver transmitter (UART) is a common asynchronous functional unit found in most modern computer systems. UARTs are used extensively when computers communicate with serial devices such as printers and terminals, but they are also applied when the number of connection lines needs to be minimized (at the expense of speed). The two main functions of a UART are: 1) take a parallel data word in from the computer and write it out serially and, 2) read in serial external data and convert it to a parallel word for the computer.

The serial-in parallel-out operation is initiated by a negative transition on the serial data input that is held low for over a half of a clock period. The half period time mark is used then used to clock in a data word (8 bits in this example); when an entire word is received, the completion signal NINTI is set low until the data word has been read.

The parallel-in serial-out operation is initiated by a positive transition of the LOAD signal. Completion of the serial-out operation is signalled via the low state of NINTO. A common parallel word interface port, DATA, is used for external input of parallel-in data and parallel-out data.

The operation characteristics of the UART it make it an ideal example for showing how to approach an asynchronous design problem. The remainder of this section focuses on the design and implementation of a simple 8-bit UART. The UART design example is based on the Chapter 5 UART example in James Armstrong's book "Chip-Level Modeling with VHDL" (Prentice-Hall 1989).

The design problem is most easily understood when approached hierarchically. The UART will be broken into four major functional subunits:

Functional Subunits of UARTs

PAR_IN_SER_OUT - parallel-in serial-out operation
SER_IN_PAR_OUT - serial-in parallel-out operation
CLOCK_GEN   - clock generator
BTS4_BANK   - bidirectional I/O control

The project package lays some of the foundational work for the network description. We can set the word length by using a VHDL constant in the package. Although the DATA port of the design is bidirectional, we can still use the type bit as the base data type for the system; to have multiple drivers (sources) on a signal a bus resolution function (BRF) must be defined for simulation purposes. The BRF can be ignored by the synthesis tool in this case because a simple wired connection is all that is actually needed (connect of all sources). It is also convenient to put all of the component statements into the package so that they do not have to be repeated throughout the code.

```
package TSL_Package is
  constant WORD_LENGTH : integer := 8;
  subtype WORD  is BIT_VECTOR((WORD_LENGTH-1)
        downto 0);
  type WORD_VECTOR is array (INTEGER RANGE <>) of
        WORD;
  function WIRED_OR(SOURCES: BIT_VECTOR)
        return bit;
  function WIRED_OR(SOURCES: WORD_VECTOR)
        return WORD;

  component CLOCK_GEN
  -- Synopsys TRANSLATE_OFF
  generic (ICLK_DEL, OCLK_DEL : Time);
  -- Synopsys TRANSLATE_ON
  port( ICLK : buffer BIT;
      OCLK : buffer BIT);
  end component;
```

```
component BTS4
port( A: in  BIT; E: in  BIT; Z: out wired_or BIT);
end component;

component BTS4_BANK
port( IN_WORD : in  WORD; ENABLE  : in  BIT;
    OUT_WORD: out wired_or WORD);
end component;

component PAR_IN_SER_OUT
port (DATA: in  WORD; LOAD: in  bit; CLOCK: in  bit;
    NINTO: out bit; O: out bit);
end component;

component SER_IN_PAR_OUT
port (I: in  BIT; CLOCK: in  bit; NINTI: buffer bit;
    OUTPUT: out WORD);
end component;

component UART
-- Synopsys TRANSLATE_OFF
generic (Clk_Per,ODel,INDel,INTDel: Time := 0 ns);
-- Synopsys TRANSLATE_ON
port ( DATA: inout WORD; I: in BIT; LOAD: in BIT;
    READ: in BIT;
    O: out BIT; NINTO: out BIT; NINTI: buffer BIT);
end component;
end TSL_Package;

package body TSL_Package is
 function WIRED_OR( SOURCES: BIT_VECTOR)
        return BIT is
begin
  -- Synopsys TRANSLATE_OFF
  for I in SOURCES'LEFT to SOURCES'RIGHT LOOP
   if SOURCES(I) = BIT' ('1') then return BIT' ('1'); end if;
  end loop;
  return BIT' ('0');
```

```
  -- Synopsys TRANSLATE_ON
  end WIRED_OR;

function WIRED_OR(SOURCES: WORD_VECTOR)
        return WORD is
   variable RESOLVED_WORD : WORD;
  begin
    for BIT_INDEX in WORD'LOW to WORD'HIGH loop
     RESOLVED_WORD(BIT_INDEX) := '0';
     for WORD_INDEX in SOURCES'LEFT to
          SOURCES'RIGHT loop
      if(SOURCES(WORD_INDEX)(BIT_INDEX) = '1')
then
         RESOLVED_WORD(BIT_INDEX) := '1';
      end if;
     end loop;
    end loop;
    return RESOLVED_WORD;
  end WIRED_OR;
end TSL_Package;
```

The bidirectional data port requires the use of a three-state element that is drawn from the technology library. This cell is then used within a bank (whose width is determined by the WORD_LENGTH constant) that is created via the generate statement. The model of the primitive cell has been included to show how a simple model can be created. Note however that error checking for three-state contention is not possible with this model. Because the cell is a library primitive, we can turn off synthesis translation around this component (via — Synopsys TRANS-LATE_OFF meta-com-ment). The resultant network is a hierarchical instantiation of the three-state driver network.

```
  -- Synopsys TRANSLATE_OFF
use work.TSL_Package.all;
  entity BTS4 is
   port( A  : in  BIT;         -- data input
         E  : in  BIT;         -- enable
         Z  : out wired_or BIT);  -- resolved bit data
output
   end BTS4;

  architecture BTS4_HDL of BTS4 is
  begin
    process (A,E)
    begin
     if (E = '0') then Z <= '0';
  -- 3stated state is zero here!!
     else Z <= A;
     end if;
    end process;
   end BTS4_HDL;
   -- Synopsys TRANSLATE_ON

use work.TSL_Package.all;
  entity BTS4_BANK is
   port( IN_WORD : in  WORD;
        ENABLE  : in  BIT;
        OUT_WORD: out WORD);
   end BTS4_BANK;

  architecture BTS4_BANK_RTL of BTS4_BANK is
  begin
   GEN_BANK : for I in WORD_LENGTH-1 downto 0
generate
     U1 : BTS4 port map(IN_WORD(I), ENABLE,
       OUT_WORD(I));
    end generate;
   end BTS4_BANK_RTL;
```

As mentioned in the Explicit Timing section of this chapter, clock generation is not a generally synthesizable part of the overall design. For this project, we have created a special entity that generates both the input and output clocks of the system. Again, for illustrative purposes, we have included the simulation model portions of this design surrounded by synthesis meta-comments to turn off and on the processing of the model.

```
entity CLOCK_GEN is
  -- Synopsys TRANSLATE_OFF
  generic (ICLK_DEL, OCLK_DEL : Time := 0 ns);
  -- Synopsys TRANSLATE_ON
  port( ICLK : buffer BIT;
      OCLK : buffer BIT);
end CLOCK_GEN;

architecture CLOCK_GEN_RTL of CLOCK_GEN is
  signal tmp_ICLK, tmp_OCLK : BIT;
begin
  -- Synopsys TRANSLATE_OFF
  process(tmp_ICLK,tmp_OCLK) begin
    tmp_ICLK <= not tmp_ICLK after ICLK_DEL/4;
    tmp_OCLK <= not tmp_OCLK after OCLK_DEL;
  end process;
  ICLK <= tmp_ICLK;
  OCLK <= tmp_OCLK;
  -- Synopsys TRANSLATE_ON
end CLOCK_GEN_RTL;
```

The outcome of the synthesis process for the clock network is the instantiation of the CLOCK_GEN entity.

The parallel-in serial-out block is based on a WORD_LENGTH +1 length shift register. The shift register is loaded with the input data word and an extra 1 at the top bit. As the word is shifted down, it is zero filled. When the top WORD_LENGTH bits are all zero, then shifting is complete and the completion signal is sent. Note that the completion signal generated is for this module, and not the final signal sent to the UART output (see the top-level module description for the use of the submodule completion signal).

```
--
-- Parallel-In Serial-Out Converter
--
use work.TSL_Package.all;
entity PAR_IN_SER_OUT is
  port (DATA : in  WORD;
      LOAD : in  bit;
      CLOCK : in  bit;
      NINTO : out bit;
      O    : out bit
      );
end PAR_IN_SER_OUT;

architecture PAR_IN_SER_OUT_RTL of
PAR_IN_SER_OUT is
  signal OREG, NEXT_OREG : bit_vector
(WORD_LENGTH downto 0);
begin
```

```
-- if LOAD then parallel load, else store next state
SEQ_PAR_IN :
process(LOAD,CLOCK,DATA,NEXT_OREG)
 begin
  if (LOAD = bit' ('1')) then
   OREG <= (bit' ('1') & DATA);
  elsif (CLOCK'event and CLOCK = '1') then
   OREG <= NEXT_OREG;
  end if;
 end process;
 -- compute next state, and the completion signal
COM_PAR_IN : process(OREG)
  variable go : bit;
 begin
  go := bit' ('0');
  for I in WORD_LENGTH downto 1 loop
   go := go or OREG(I);
  end loop;
  NINTO <= go;
  NEXT_OREG <= bit' ('0') &
OREG(WORD_LENGTH downto 1);
  O <= OREG(0);
 end process;
end PAR_IN_SER_OUT_RTL;
```

The schematic for the synthesized model PAR_IN_SER_OUT is shown below. Note that the implementation has, in this case, been very tightly controlled by the explicit use of a shift register architecture based description.

The serial-in parallel-out operation performed in the submodule SER_IN_PAR_OUT uses a shift register architecture similar to the parallel-in module. This module receives a clock from the CLOCK_GEN module that runs four times the speed of the desired input rate; this clock can then be used as the basis for sampling, and divided and used for shifting operation. Embedded in the model is a state machine that watches for the low transition of the data input I, and makes sure that the input is low for two additional clock ticks before sampling begins. An enumerated type has been declared for the state machine's state values. The completion signal, NINTI, is also controlled within the state machine process.

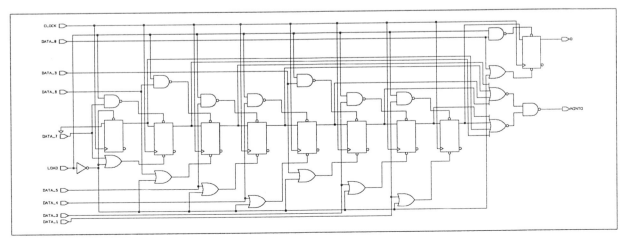

```
--
-- Serial-In Parallel-Out Converter
-- (clock input is 4x clock for operation to set sample time)
--
use work.TSL_Package.all;
  entity SER_IN_PAR_OUT is
    port (I: in  bit;
        CLOCK: in  bit;
        NINTI: buffer bit;
        OUTPUT: out WORD);
  end SER_IN_PAR_OUT;

    architecture SER_IN_PAR_OUT_RTL of
SER_IN_PAR_OUT is
    -- enum type for FSM
    type I_STATE is (RESET_STATE, I_LOW_1, I_LOW_2,
            I_LOW_3, RUNNING);
    signal STATE, NEXT_STATE : I_STATE;
    signal IREG : bit_vector (WORD_LENGTH downto 0);
    signal DIV_CLOCK, RESET, RUNNING_STATE : bit;

    begin
    -- clock dividing process - divide by four
    DIVIDE_CLOCK : process
    variable STATE : integer range 0 to 3;
    begin
      wait until CLOCK'event and CLOCK = '1';
        if (STATE < 3) then
          STATE := STATE + 1;
          DIV_CLOCK <= '0';
        else
          STATE := 0;
          DIV_CLOCK <= RUNNING_STATE;
        end if;
    end process;

    -- shift register process with asynch clear to 0...01
    SHIFT_IN : process(DIV_CLOCK)

    begin
      if (RESET = '1') then
        IREG(WORD_LENGTH downto 1) <= "00000000";
        IREG(0) <= '1';
      elsif (DIV_CLOCK'event and DIV_CLOCK = '1') then
        IREG <= IREG(WORD_LENGTH-1 downto 0) & I;
      end if;
    end process;

    -- output get low word_length bits
    OUTPUT <= IREG(WORD_LENGTH-1 downto 0);
    -- state machine state register declaration
    SAVE_STATE : process begin
      wait until CLOCK'event and CLOCK = '1';
        STATE <= NEXT_STATE;
    end process;

    -- find low I bit (low for half period = 2 more ticks
    FIND_START : process(I,STATE,IREG)
    begin
      case STATE is
        when RESET_STATE =>
            if (I = '0') then NEXT_STATE <= I_LOW_1;
            else           NEXT_STATE <= RESET_STATE;
            end if;
            NINTI <= '1';
        when I_LOW_1 =>
            if (I = '0') then NEXT_STATE <= I_LOW_2;
            else           NEXT_STATE <= RESET_STATE;
            end if;
            NINTI <= '1';
        when I_LOW_2 =>
            if (I = '0') then NEXT_STATE <= I_LOW_3;
            else           NEXT_STATE <= RESET_STATE;
            end if;
            NINTI <= '1';
        when I_LOW_3 =>
```

```vhdl
       if (I = '0') then NEXT_STATE <= RUNNING;
       else          NEXT_STATE <= RESET_STATE;
       end if;
       NINTI <= '1';
   when RUNNING =>
       if (IREG(WORD_LENGTH) = '0') then
        NEXT_STATE <= RUNNING;
        NINTI <= '1';
       else
        NEXT_STATE <= RESET_STATE;
        NINTI <= '0';
       end if;
   end case;

   if (STATE = RUNNING) then
     RESET <= '0';
     RUNNING_STATE <= '1';
   else
     RESET <= '1';
     RUNNING_STATE <= '0';
   end if;
end process;


end SER_IN_PAR_OUT_RTL;
```

The schematic for the synthesized serial-in to parallel-out converter is shown below. With the major functional units described, the top level description requires component instantiation and a little bit of glue logic to generate the final completion signal for the serial input operation.

```vhdl
use work.TSL_Package.all;
entity UART is
  -- Synopsys TRANSLATE_OFF
  generic (Clk_Per, ODel, INDel, INTDel : Time := 0 fs);
  -- Synopsys TRANSLATE_ON
  port ( DATA  : inout wired_or WORD;
      I    : in  bit;
      LOAD : in  bit;
      READ : in  bit;
      O    : out  bit;
      NINTO : out  bit;
      NINTI : buffer bit);
end UART;
```

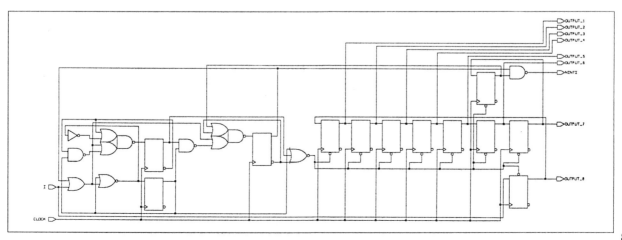

```
architecture RTL of UART is
    signal ICLK, OCLK : bit;
    signal IREG : WORD;
    signal GATED_OCLK, NINTI_1, TMP_NINTI : bit;
begin

 GATED_OCLK <= LOAD and OCLK;
 NINTI <= TMP_NINTI;

 NINIT_I_BIT : process(READ,NINTI_1,ICLK)  begin
  if (READ = '1' or NINTI_1 = '1') then
   if (READ = '1')      then TMP_NINTI <= '1';
   elsif (NINTI_1 = '1') then TMP_NINTI <= '0';
   end if;
  elsif (ICLK'event and ICLK = '1') then
   TMP_NINTI <= TMP_NINTI;
  end if;
 end process;

 U1 : BTS4_BANK port map(IREG,READ,DATA);

 U2 : CLOCK_GEN
    -- Synopsys TRANSLATE_OFF
    generic map (INDel,ODel)
    -- Synopsys TRANSLATE_ON
    port map(ICLK,OCLK);

 U3 : PAR_IN_SER_OUT port
map(DATA,LOAD,GATED_OCLK,NINTO,O);

 U4 : SER_IN_PAR_OUT port map(I,ICLK,NINTI_1,IREG);
end RTL;
```

The top level schematic (shown below) shows the remainder of the UART implementation. Asynchronous operation is an important aspect of HDL-based design. The descriptive capabilities of the synthesis policy provide sufficient power to write asynchronous and synchronous models.

Top-Level Schematic of UART Implementation

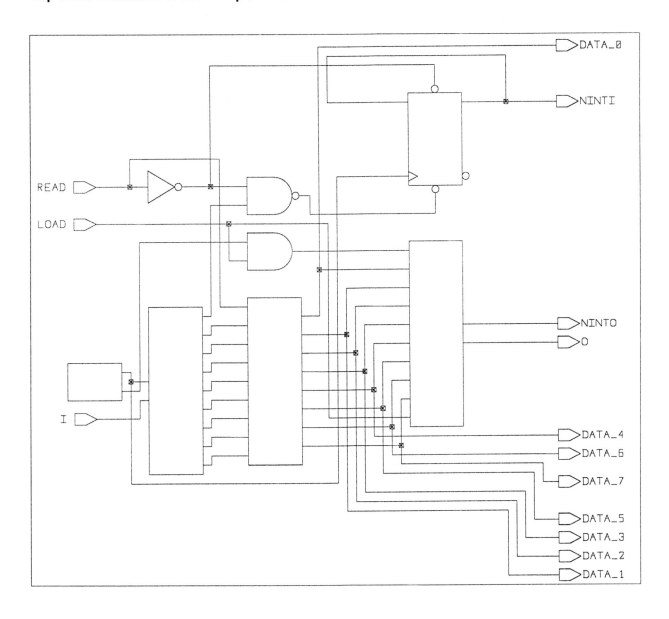

6

Synthesizing the AM2910A

In this chapter the HDL design methodology is applied to Advanced Micro Devices' AM2910A microcontroller. The chapter begins with a brief overview of the AM2910A, and then delves into the individual modules of the design. Some of the basics of the usage of VHDL packages are included to show how a project team might share VHDL code. The chapter completes with the results of the synthesis process for the entire design.

The 2910 Architecture

The AM2910A is a 12-bit microcontroller that is an address sequencer intended for controlling the sequence of execution of microinstructions stored in micro-program memory. It has been designed to be used in conjunction with a micro-program memory, status registers, ALU's, and other similar building blocks to create custom microcontroller architectures.

The device uses a 12-bit internal data path that allows the external addressing of up to 4K words of microprogram. The controller contains a four input multiplexer that allows the selection of the stack, a register/counter, microprogram counter, or an external source as the next address. The stack is 9 words deep and has an overflow detect external output. The register counter is used primarily for setting up loops, and has a zero detect signal for this purpose. The microprogram register is used as the stack input for subroutine linkage, and generation of sequential address values. The device architecture, taken from the AMD data-book, is shown on the facing page.

Designing the 2910

When approaching the HDL design methodology, one should begin by thinking of functional design rather than language based design. The mind-set of functional design is characterized by conscious usage of functional units rather than sequential algorithmic behavior. The design of the 2910 is taken forward by choosing the major functional units that will be used in concert to produce the desired functionality; rather than an approach where a subroutine is written for every instruction. We want to have a target architecture in mind during the RTL model writing stage.

When designing the 2910, the architecture outlined by the AMD data-sheet is a useful starting point. This data sheet suggests the creation of five major functional units: the instruction decoder (CONTROL), a data multiplexor (Y), a register counter (REGCNT), a microprogram count (UPC), and a stack (STACK) module. A single clock input to the system will allow us to use a simple, edge triggered, synchronous-clocking methodology. The one feature of the 2910 ignored is the three-state output that serves no purpose in our target system.

The design process then proceeds a module at a time. As each design unit's RTL description is completed, a simulation is performed to validate the functional behavior.

AMD 2910 Architecture

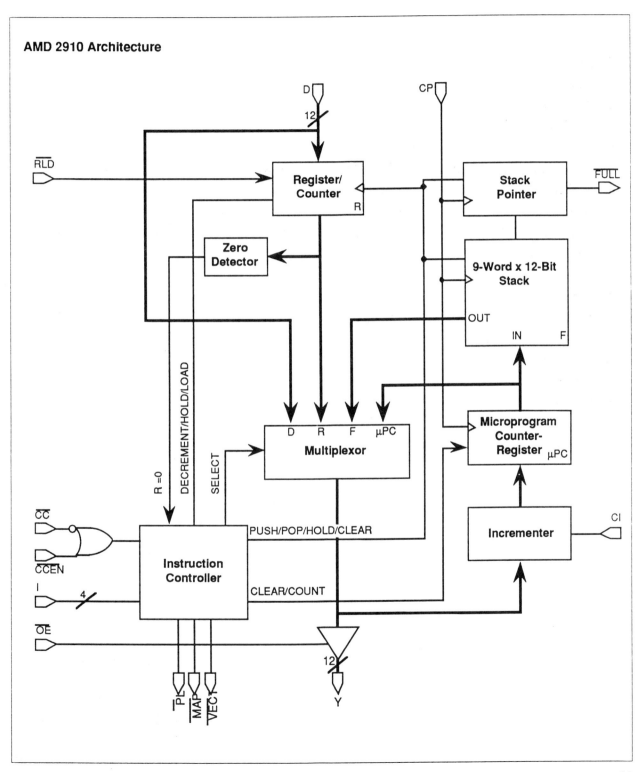

To perform the simulations, a test driver is written for each module. The test module is written as a "wrapper" for the module to be tested. The test driver instantiates one instance of the module to be tested, and has signals connecting to each of the module I/O ports. The signals attached to the input ports are driven to provide the device input stimulus, and the output signals are monitored for expected results.

The following five sections introduce each of the modules, and show the results of the functional validation. In each of the modules we are drawing on declarations that are made in a project package (AMD_PACK), and the Synopsys standard package (SYNOPSYS). You may want to skip ahead to the sections describing the contents of the packages.

Selected signal assignment builds next-address multiplexor

Y.vhd

The "Y" module of the Am2910 serves as a multiplexer that passes the selected input to the "Y" bus. The inputs to the multiplexer are from the data input bus (D) , the register/counter module (REGCNT) , the nine word stack pointer module (STACK), or the microprogram counter module (UPC). It is also possible to select none of the inputs and get a zero at the output. The instruction PLA module (CONTROL) controls the multiplexer. In VHDL it is very convenient to use selected signal assignment to represent a multiplexing structure that is based on a single (possibly multiple bit) control variable.

```
use work.SYNOPSYS.all;
use work.AMD_PACK.all;
entity Y is
  port(OPERATION : in Y_MUX_OPS;
     DATA_IN   : in ADDRESS;
     REGCNT_IN : in ADDRESS;
     STACK_IN  : in ADDRESS;
     UPC_IN    : in ADDRESS;
     MUXOUT    : out ADDRESS);
end Y;
architecture Y_HDL of Y is
begin
  with OPERATION select
   MUXOUT <= DATA_IN
     when SELECT_DATA,REGCNT_IN
     when SELECT_REGCNT, STACK_IN
     when SELECT_STACK, UPC_IN
     when SELECT_UPC, ADDRESS'(others => '0')
     when SELECT_NONE;
end Y_HDL;
```

The simulation test driver for this module is shown below to illustrate the approach we have taken to the RTL validation step. With the exception of the top level design (the entire AM2910), all of the modules were validated with test drivers of the same structure.

```
-- TEST DRIVER FOR Y

use work.SYNOPSYS.all ;
use work.AMD_PACK.all ;

-- Test driver entity has no ports - it's just a wrapper
entity test_y is
end test_y;

use work.SYNOPSYS.all ;
use work.AMD_PACK.all ;
architecture y_arch of test_y is

-- Component declaration for the module Y
 component Y port(
     OPERATION : in Y_MUX_OPS;  DATA_IN
               : in ADDRESS ;
     REGCNT_IN : in ADDRESS ;  STACK_IN
               : in ADDRESS ;
     UPC_IN    : in ADDRESS ;  MUXOUT
               : out ADDRESS) ;
end component;

-- Signals to connect to the ports of Y
 signal MY_DATA_IN, MY_REGCNT_IN, MY_STACK_IN,
     MY_UPC_IN,
     MY_MUXOUT : ADDRESS := X"000";
 signal MY_OPERATION : Y_MUX_OPS :=
     SELECT_NONE;

begin
     -- Data values for each signal source
     MY_DATA_IN   <= X"800";
     MY_REGCNT_IN <= X"400";
     MY_STACK_IN  <= X"200";
     MY_UPC_IN    <= X"100";

-- Process to apply all of the control values of Y
  process
  begin
-- Try selecting each of the operations
    MY_OPERATION <= SELECT_DATA;   wait for 10 ns;
--time 0
    MY_OPERATION <= SELECT_REGCNT; wait for 10 ns;
--time 10
    MY_OPERATION <= SELECT_STACK;  wait for 10 ns;
--time 20
    MY_OPERATION <= SELECT_UPC;    wait for 10 ns;
--time 30
    MY_OPERATION <= SELECT_NONE;   wait for 10 ns;
--time 40
  end process;

-- Instantiate the Y module
  U0 : Y port map (MY_OPERATION, MY_DATA_IN,
          MY_REGCNT_IN,
          MY_STACK_IN, MY_UPC_IN,
          MY_MUXOUT);
end y_arch;
```

Simulation of the VHDL description of the Y (multiplexer) block reveals the following expected I/O response:

Upc.vhd

The microprogram counter (UPC) module is composed of a 12-bit incrementer followed by a 12-bit register. The UPC can be used in either of two ways when the OPERATION input port has a value COUNT: When the carry-in to the incrementer is HIGH, the microprogram register is loaded on the next clock cycle with the current Y output word plus one (Y + 1 => UPC). Sequential microinstructions are thus executed. When the carry-in is LOW, the incrementer passes the Y output word unmodified so that the mPC is reloaded with the same Y word on the next clock cycle (Y => UPC). When the value of the input port OPERATION has the value CLEAR, then OUTPUT is set to zero. The same microinstruction is executed any number of times.

Here we will use the VHDL wait statement to model the registered behavior of the UPC module. The predefined attribute, stable, of a signal allows the monitoring of a signal for a change; the check for CLOCK='1' ensures that the change is a rising transition. Because there are only two basic operations to the UPC module, we can use an if-else structure to describe the module behavior.

```
0 nS
    MY_DATA_IN    = X"800"
 -- set data value to 800 hex
    MY_REGCNT_IN  = X"400"
 -- set regcnt value to 400 hex
    MY_STACK_IN   = X"200"
 -- set the stack value to 200 hex
    MY_UPC_IN     = X"100"
 -- set the upc value to 100 hex
    MY_OPERATION  = SELECT_DATA
 -- select data input
    MY_MUXOUT     = X"000"
    MY_MUXOUT     = X"800"

10 nS
    MY_OPERATION  = SELECT_REGCNT
 -- select regcnt input
    MY_MUXOUT     = X"400"

20 nS
    MY_OPERATION  = SELECT_STACK
 -- select stack input
    MY_MUXOUT     = X"200"

30 nS
    MY_OPERATION  = SELECT_UPC
 -- select upc input
    MY_MUXOUT     = X"100"

40 nS
    MY_OPERATION  = SELECT_NONE
 -- select nothing
    MY_MUXOUT     = X"000"
 -- output
```

```
use work.SYNOPSYS.all;
use work.AMD_PACK.all;

entity UPC is
  port( OPERATION  : in UPC_OPS;
         DATA : in ADDRESS;
         CARRY_IN  : in BIT;
         CLOCK  : in BIT;
         OUTPUT  : buffer ADDRESS;
         OUTPUT_BAR : out ADDRESS);
end UPC;

architecture UPC_HDL of UPC is
begin
  process
  begin
    -- Wait for a rising clock edge before doing anything
    wait until (not CLOCK'stable and CLOCK = '1');
    if OPERATION = COUNT then
      OUTPUT <= DATA + CARRY_IN;
    else
      OUTPUT <= ADDRESS'(others => '0');
    end if;
  end process;

  OUTPUT_BAR <= not OUTPUT;
end UPC_HDL;
```

Wait statement implies registers to store the program counter

Two operations: CLEAR and COUNT

Simulation of the µPC block reveals the following expected behavior:

0 nS
```
MY_OPERATION  = COUNT
MY_DATA       = X"CCC"
-- set input data to CCC hex
MY_OUTPUT_BAR = X"FFF"
-- out bar remains complement
```

10 nS
```
MY_CLOCK      = '1'
MY_OUT_PUT    = X"000"
```
20 nS
```
MY_CLOCK      = '0'
```

30 nS
```
MY_OPERATION  = COUNT
-- set operation variable to count
```

40 nS
```
MY_CLOCK      = '1'
MY_OUT_PUT    = X"CCC"
-- output becomes input
MY_OUTPUT_BAR = X"333"
```

50 nS
```
MY_CLOCK      = '0'
```

60 nS
```
MY_CARRY_IN   = '1'
```

70 nS
```
MY_CLOCK      = '1'
MY_OUT_PUT    = X"CCD"
-- output becomes one plus input value
MY_OUTPUT_BAR = X"332"
-- output bar becomes valid
```

Regcnt.vhd

REGCNT is controlled by the input OPERATION. If OPERATION is LOAD, the input is written directly to the output. If it is DECREMENT, the old output is decremented. If it is NOOP, the old output is preserved. Since we need to preserve the value of output from one cycle to the next, the "wait" construct was used. The output ZERO is computed using the BIT_OF function from the SYNOPSYS package; this function converts the boolean result of the comparison to a bit value.

```
use work.SYNOPSYS.all;
use work.AMD_PACK.all;

entity REGCNT is
  port(OPERATION : in REGCNT_OPS;
       DATA      : in ADDRESS;
       CLOCK     : in BIT;
       OUTPUT    : buffer ADDRESS;
       ZERO      : out BIT);
end REGCNT;
architecture REGCNT_HDL of REGCNT is
begin
```

Three operations: LOAD, DECREMENT, NO_OP
Wait implies register to hold current value

```
process
begin
  wait until not CLOCK'stable and CLOCK = '1';
  if OPERATION = LOAD then
    OUTPUT <= DATA;
  elsif OPERATION = DEC then
    OUTPUT <= OUTPUT - 1;
  end if;
end process;
```

98

```
┌─────────────────────────────────────────┐
│  **Detect zero bit**                     │
└─────────────────────────────────────────┘
```

└─ ZERO <= BIT_OF(OUTPUT = ADDRESS'(others => '0'));
end REGCNT_HDL;

Simulation of the VHDL description of
REGCNT reveals the following expected   I/O
response:

-- First try loading

0 NS

　0 MY_CLOCK　　= '1'
　0 MY_ZERO　　 = '1'

10 NS

　10 MY_CLOCK　　= '0'

20 NS

　20 MY_DATA　　 = X"111"

30 NS

　30 MY_CLOCK　　= '1'

40 NS

　40 MY_CLOCK　　= '0'

50 NS

　50   MY_OPERATION = LOAD

60 NS

　60 MY_CLOCK　　= '1'
　60 MY_OUT_PUT　= X"111"
　60 MY_ZERO　　 = '0'

70 NS

　70 MY_CLOCK　　= '0'

80 NS

　80 MY_DATA　　 = X"999

90 NS

　90 MY_CLOCK　　= '1'
　90 MY_OUT_PUT　= X"999"
　90 MY_ZERO　　 = '0'

100 NS

　100 MY_CLOCK　　= '0'

110 NS

　110 MY_OPERATION = LOAD

120 NS

　120 MY_CLOCK　　= '1'
　120 MY_OUT_PUT　= X"999"

130 NS

　130 MY_CLOCK　　= '0'

-- Now let's try decrementing
140 NS

　140 MY_OPERATION = DEC

150 NS

　150 MY_CLOCK　　= '1
　150 MY_OUT_PUT　= X"998"
　150 MY_ZERO　　 = '0'

160 NS

　160 MY_CLOCK　　= '0'

170 NS

　170 MY_CLOCK　　= '1'
　170 MY_OUT_PUT　= X"997"
　170 MY_ZERO　　 = '0'

180 NS

180 MY_CLOCK   = '0'

190 NS

190 MY_CLOCK   = '1'
190 MY_OUT_PUT = X"996"
190 MY_ZERO   = '0'

200 NS

200 MY_CLOCK   = '0'
210 NS
210 MY_DATA   = X"333"

220 NS

220 MY_CLOCK   = '1'
220 MY_OUT_PUT = X"995"
220 MY_ZERO   = '0'

230 NS

230 MY_CLOCK   = '0'
-- Let's load a new value

240 NS

240   MY_OPERATION = LOAD

250 NS

250 MY_CLOCK   = '1'
250 MY_OUT_PUT = X"333"
250 MY_ZERO   = '0'

260 NS

260 MY_CLOCK   = '0'

270 NS

270 MY_CLOCK   = '1'
270 MY_OUT_PUT = X"333"

280 NS

280 MY_CLOCK   = '0'

100

Control.vhd

The Control module of the Am2910 serves
as an instruction decoder and multiplexer for
the other modules in the design. The controller stores no information, so it does not
contain a wait statement. The controller
outputs depend on the instruction and some
condition code values. It is implemented
with a single case statement that switches on
the value of the instruction input. Each
alternative of the case implements one of the
instructions. This is by far the most complex VHDL module in the 2910. However,
the description style used here yields a
model that is quite straightforward to code
and understand.

```
entity CONTROL is
  port(INSTRUCTION          : in INSTRUCTION_OPS;
     CONDITION_CODE     : in BIT;
     CONDITION_CODE_ENABLE   : in BIT;
     FORCE_LOAD         : in BIT;
     REGCNT_ZERO        : in BIT;
     UPC_CONTROL        : out UPC_OPS;
     STACK_CONTROL      : out STACK_OPS;
     REGCNT_CONTROL : out REGCNT_OPS;
     Y_CONTROL          : out Y_MUX_OPS;
     PIPELINE_ENABLE    : out BIT;
     MAPPING_ROM_ENABLE     : out BIT;
     INTERRUPT_VECTOR_ENABLE : out BIT);
end CONTROL;

architecture CONTROL_HDL of CONTROL is
begin
CONTROL_LOGIC: process( INSTRUCTION,
           CONDITION_CODE,
           CONDITION_CODE_ENABLE,
```

```
FORCE_LOAD,REGCNT_ZERO)
  begin
    -- give default values to outputs
```

```
┌─────────────────────────────────────────────┐
│  Set default values for control outputs     │
└─────────────────────────────────────────────┘
```

```
    PIPELINE_ENABLE    <= '1';
    MAPPING_ROM_ENABLE <= '1';
    INTERRUPT_VECTOR_ENABLE <= '1';
    UPC_CONTROL   <= COUNT;
    STACK_CONTROL <= S_NOOP;
    Y_CONTROL     <= SELECT_UPC;
    -- watch for the force load signal input
    if( FORCE_LOAD = '1') then
      REGCNT_CONTROL <= NOOP;
    else
      REGCNT_CONTROL <= LOAD;
    end if;
    case INSTRUCTION is
      -- Reset: clear stack and upc
      when JZ =>
        UPC_CONTROL <= CLEAR;
        STACK_CONTROL <= S_CLEAR;
        Y_CONTROL <= SELECT_NONE;
        PIPELINE_ENABLE <= '0';
```

```
┌─────────────────────────────────────────────┐
│  Interpret instruction using VHDL case      │
│  statement                                   │
└─────────────────────────────────────────────┘
```

```
    -- Cond jump sub: either jump on data in or do next
inst
      when CJS =>
        PIPELINE_ENABLE <= '0';
        if not (CONDITION_CODE_ENABLE = '0' and
              CONDITION_CODE = '1') then
          STACK_CONTROL <= S_PUSH;
          Y_CONTROL <= SELECT_DATA;
        end if;
```

```
      -- Jump using map:
      when JMAP =>
        MAPPING_ROM_ENABLE <= '0';
        Y_CONTROL <= SELECT_DATA;

      -- Cond jump: either jump or next inst
      when CJP =>
        PIPELINE_ENABLE <= '0';
        if not (CONDITION_CODE_ENABLE = '0' and
              CONDITION_CODE = '1') then
            Y_CONTROL <= SELECT_DATA;
          end if;

      -- Push stack: stack gets next inst addr
      when PUSH =>
        STACK_CONTROL <= S_PUSH;
        PIPELINE_ENABLE <= '0';
        if not (CONDITION_CODE_ENABLE = '0' and
              CONDITION_CODE = '1') then
            REGCNT_CONTROL <= LOAD;
        end if;

      -- Push and cond jump sub (2-way)
      when JSRP =>
        PIPELINE_ENABLE <= '0';
        STACK_CONTROL <= S_PUSH;
        if (CONDITION_CODE_ENABLE = '0' and
            CONDITION_CODE = '1') then
            Y_CONTROL <= SELECT_REGCNT;
        else
          Y_CONTROL <= SELECT_DATA;
          end if;
      -- Cond junk using vector interrupt
      when CJV =>
        INTERRUPT_VECTOR_ENABLE <= '0';
        if not (CONDITION_CODE_ENABLE = '0' and
              CONDITION_CODE = '1') then
```

```
      Y_CONTROL <= SELECT_DATA;          -- Conditional jump and pop
        end if;                          when CJPP =>
-- Cond jump (2-way)                      PIPELINE_ENABLE <= '0';
when JRP =>                               if not (CONDITION_CODE_ENABLE = '0' and
 PIPELINE_ENABLE <= '0';                      CONDITION_CODE = '1') then
 if (CONDITION_CODE_ENABLE = '0' and          Y_CONTROL <= SELECT_DATA;
   CONDITION_CODE = '1') then                 STACK_CONTROL <= S_POP;
   Y_CONTROL <= SELECT_REGCNT;          end if;
 else
   Y_CONTROL <= SELECT_DATA;            -- Load counter/register
  end if;                              when LDCT =>
                                         PIPELINE_ENABLE <= '0';
                                         REGCNT_CONTROL <= LOAD;
-- Repeat stack loop if cntr != '0'
when RFCT =>                             -- Test end of loop
 PIPELINE_ENABLE <= '0';               when LOP =>
 if( REGCNT_ZERO = '0') then             PIPELINE_ENABLE <= '0';
   Y_CONTROL <= SELECT_STACK;           if (CONDITION_CODE_ENABLE = '0' and
       REGCNT_CONTROL <= DEC;               CONDITION_CODE = '1') then
 else                                        Y_CONTROL <= SELECT_STACK;
   STACK_CONTROL <= S_POP;             -- test failed
  end if;                               else
                                            STACK_CONTROL <= S_POP;
                                        -- end loop and pop
-- Repeat D loop is cntr != 0              end if;
when RPCT =>
 PIPELINE_ENABLE <= '0';                -- Continue, no-op
 if( REGCNT_ZERO = '0') then           when CONT =>PIPELINE_ENABLE <= '0';
     Y_CONTROL <= SELECT_DATA;
     REGCNT_CONTROL <= DEC;             -- Three-way branch
  end if;                              when TWB =>
                                         PIPELINE_ENABLE <= '0';
                                         if( REGCNT_ZERO = '0') then
-- Conditional return                     REGCNT_CONTROL <= DEC;
when CRTN =>                                 if (CONDITION_CODE_ENABLE = '0' and
 PIPELINE_ENABLE <= '0';                         CONDITION_CODE = '1') then
 if not (CONDITION_CODE_ENABLE = '0' and        Y_CONTROL <= SELECT_STACK;
       CONDITION_CODE = '1') then             else
       Y_CONTROL <= SELECT_STACK;
       STACK_CONTROL <= S_POP;
  end if;
```

```
            STACK_CONTROL <= S_POP;
        end if;
    else
        STACK_CONTROL <= S_POP;
        if (CONDITION_CODE_ENABLE = '0' and
            CONDITION_CODE = '1') then
        Y_CONTROL <= SELECT_DATA;
    end if;
        end if;
  end case;
 end process CONTROL_LOGIC;
end CONTROL_HDL;
```

Simulation of the VHDL description of
CONTROL shows the following expected
I/O response:

```
-- Set CONDITION_CODE to 1
0 NS
0   MY_CONDITION_CODE        = '1'
0   MY_PIPELINE_ENABLE       = '0'
0   MY_REGCNT_CONTROL        = LOAD
0   MY_Y_CONTROL             = SELECT_UPC
0   MY_STACK_CONTROL         = S_NOOP
0   MY_UPC_CONTROL           = COUNT
0   MY_INTERRUPT_VECTOR_ENABLE  = '1'
0   MY_MAPPING_ROM_ENABLE       = '1'
0   MY_PIPELINE_ENABLE       = '0'
0   MY_REGCNT_CONTROL        = LOAD
0   MY_Y_CONTROL             = SELECT_UPC
0   MY_STACK_CONTROL         = S_NOOP
0   MY_UPC_CONTROL           = COUNT
0   MY_INTERRUPT_VECTOR_ENABLE  = '1'
0   MY_MAPPING_ROM_ENABLE       = '1'
```

```
--Set CONDITION_CODE to 0
10 NS
10   MY_CONDITION_CODE       = '0'
10   MY_PIPELINE_ENABLE      = '0'
10   MY_REGCNT_CONTROL       = LOAD
10   MY_Y_CONTROL            = SELECT_UPC
10   MY_STACK_CONTROL        = S_NOOP
10   MY_UPC_CONTROL          = COUNT
10   MY_INTERRUPT_VECTOR_ENABLE = '1'
10   MY_MAPPING_ROM_ENABLE      = '1'
```

```
--Set  CONDITION_CODE_ENABLE to 1
20 NS
20   MY_CONDITION_CODE_ENABLE   = '1'
20   MY_PIPELINE_ENABLE      = '0'
20   MY_REGCNT_CONTROL       = LOAD
20   MY_Y_CONTROL             = SELECT_UPC
20   MY_STACK_CONTROL        = S_NOOP
20   MY_UPC_CONTROL           = COUNT
20   MY_INTERRUPT_VECTOR_ENABLE = '1'
20   MY_MAPPING_ROM_ENABLE      = '1'
```

```
--Set CONDITION_CODE_ENABLE to 0
30 NS
30   MY_CONDITION_CODE_ENABLE   = '0'
30   MY_PIPELINE_ENABLE      = '0'
30   MY_REGCNT_CONTROL          = LOAD
30   MY_Y_CONTROL            = SELECT_UPC
30   MY_STACK_CONTROL        = S_NOOP
30   MY_UPC_CONTROL          = COUNT
30   MY_INTERRUPT_VECTOR_ENABLE = '1'
30   MY_MAPPING_ROM_ENABLE      = '1'
```

```
--Set FORCE_LOAD to 1
40 NS
40   MY_FORCE_LOAD           = '1'
40   MY_PIPELINE_ENABLE      = '0'
40   MY_REGCNT_CONTROL       = NOOP
```

```
40      MY_Y_CONTROL            = SELECT_UPC
40      MY_STACK_CONTROL        = S_NOOP
40      MY_UPC_CONTROL          = COUNT
40      MY_INTERRUPT_VECTOR_ENABLE = '1'
40      MY_MAPPING_ROM_ENABLE        = '1'


--Set FORCE_LOAD to 0
50 NS

50      MY_FORCE_LOAD           = '0'
50      MY_PIPELINE_ENABLE      = '0'
50      MY_REGCNT_CONTROL       = LOAD
50      MY_Y_CONTROL            = SELECT_UPC
50      MY_STACK_CONTROL        = S_NOOP
50      MY_UPC_CONTROL          = COUNT
50      MY_INTERRUPT_VECTOR_ENABLE = '1'
50      MY_MAPPING_ROM_ENABLE        = '1'


--Set REGCNT_ZERO to 1
60 NS

60      MY_REGCNT_ZERO          = '1'
60      MY_PIPELINE_ENABLE      = '0'
60      MY_REGCNT_CONTROL       = LOAD
60      MY_Y_CONTROL            = SELECT_UPC
60      MY_STACK_CONTROL        = S_NOOP
60      MY_UPC_CONTROL          = COUNT
60      MY_INTERRUPT_VECTOR_ENABLE = '1'
60      MY_MAPPING_ROM_ENABLE        = '1'


-- Now cycle through the entire instruction set for this
-- CONTROLLER:
70 NS

70      MY_INSTRUCTION          = JZ
70      MY_PIPELINE_ENABLE      = '0'
70      MY_Y_CONTROL            = SELECT_NONE
70      MY_STACK_CONTROL        = S_CLEAR
70      MY_UPC_CONTROL          = CLEAR
70      MY_REGCNT_CONTROL       = LOAD
```

```
70      MY_INTERRUPT_VECTOR_ENABLE = '1'
70      MY_MAPPING_ROM_ENABLE        = '1'


80 NS

80      MY_INSTRUCTION          = CJS
80      MY_Y_CONTROL            = SELECT_DATA
80      MY_STACK_CONTROL        = S_PUSH
80      MY_PIPELINE_ENABLE      = '0'
80      MY_REGCNT_CONTROL       = LOAD
80      MY_UPC_CONTROL          = COUNT
80      MY_INTERRUPT_VECTOR_ENABLE = '1'
80      MY_MAPPING_ROM_ENABLE        = '1'


90 NS

90      MY_INSTRUCTION          = JMAP
90      MY_Y_CONTROL            = SELECT_DATA
90      MY_MAPPING_ROM_ENABLE     = '0'
90      MY_REGCNT_CONTROL       = LOAD
90      MY_STACK_CONTROL        = S_NOOP
90      MY_UPC_CONTROL          = COUNT
90      MY_INTERRUPT_VECTOR_ENABLE = '1'
90      MY_PIPELINE_ENABLE      = '1'


100 NS

100     MY_INSTRUCTION          = CJP
100     MY_Y_CONTROL            = SELECT_DATA
100     MY_PIPELINE_ENABLE      = '0'
100     MY_REGCNT_CONTROL       = LOAD
100     MY_STACK_CONTROL        = S_NOOP
100     MY_UPC_CONTROL          = COUNT
100     MY_INTERRUPT_VECTOR_ENABLE = '1'
100     MY_MAPPING_ROM_ENABLE        = '1'


110 NS

110     MY_INSTRUCTION          = PUSH
110     MY_REGCNT_CONTROL       = LOAD
110     MY_PIPELINE_ENABLE      = '0'
```

110	MY_STACK_CONTROL	= S_PUSH
110	MY_Y_CONTROL	= SELECT_UPC
110	MY_UPC_CONTROL	= COUNT
110	MY_INTERRUPT_VECTOR_ENABLE = '1'	
110	MY_MAPPING_ROM_ENABLE	= '1'

120 NS

120	MY_INSTRUCTION	= JSRP
120	MY_Y_CONTROL	=SELECT_DATA
120	MY_STACK_CONTROL	= S_PUSH
120	MY_PIPELINE_ENABLE = '0'	
120	MY_REGCNT_CONTROL = LOAD	
120	MY_UPC_CONTROL	= COUNT
120	MY_INTERRUPT_VECTOR_ENABLE = '1'	
120	MY_MAPPING_ROM_ENABLE	= '1'

130 NS

130	MY_INSTRUCTION	= CJV
130	MY_Y_CONTROL	= SELECT_DATA
130	MY_INTERRUPT_VECTOR_ENABLE = '0'	
130	MY_REGCNT_CONTROL = LOAD	
130	MY_STACK_CONTROL	= S_NOOP
130	MY_UPC_CONTROL	= COUNT
130	MY_MAPPING_ROM_ENABLE	= '1'
130	MY_PIPELINE_ENABLE	= '1'

140 NS

140	MY_INSTRUCTION	= JRP
140	MY_Y_CONTROL	= SELECT_DATA
140	MY_PIPELINE_ENABLE = '0'	
140	MY_REGCNT_CONTROL	= LOAD
140	MY_STACK_CONTROL	= S_NOOP
140	MY_UPC_CONTROL	= COUNT
140	MY_INTERRUPT_VECTOR_ENABLE = '1'	
140	MY_MAPPING_ROM_ENABLE	= '1'

150 NS

150	MY_INSTRUCTION	= RFCT
150	MY_STACK_CONTROL	= S_POP
150	MY_PIPELINE_ENABLE	= '0'
150	MY_REGCNT_CONTROL	= LOAD
150	MY_Y_CONTROL	= SELECT_UPC
150	MY_UPC_CONTROL	= COUNT
150	MY_INTERRUPT_VECTOR_ENABLE = '1'	
150	MY_MAPPING_ROM_ENABLE	= '1'

160 NS

160	MY_INSTRUCTION	= RPCT
160	MY_PIPELINE_ENABLE	= '0'
160	MY_REGCNT_CONTROL	= LOAD
160	MY_Y_CONTROL	= SELECT_UPC
160	MY_STACK_CONTROL	= S_NOOP
160	MY_UPC_CONTROL	= COUNT
160	MY_INTERRUPT_VECTOR_ENABLE	= '1'
160	MY_MAPPING_ROM_ENABLE	= '1'

170 NS

170	MY_INSTRUCTION	= CRTN
170	MY_STACK_CONTROL	= S_POP
170	MY_Y_CONTROL	= SELECT_STACK
170	MY_PIPELINE_ENABLE	= '0'
170	MY_REGCNT_CONTROL	= LOAD
170	MY_UPC_CONTROL	= COUNT
170	MY_INTERRUPT_VECTOR_ENABLE	= '1'
170	MY_MAPPING_ROM_ENABLE	= '1'

180 NS

180	MY_INSTRUCTION	= CJPP
180	MY_STACK_CONTROL	= S_POP
180	MY_Y_CONTROL	= SELECT_DATA
180	MY_PIPELINE_ENABLE	= '0'
180	MY_REGCNT_CONTROL	= LOAD

180	MY_UPC_CONTROL	= COUNT
180	MY_INTERRUPT_VECTOR_ENABLE	= '1'
180	MY_MAPPING_ROM_ENABLE	= '1'

190 NS

190	MY_INSTRUCTION	= LDCT
190	MY_REGCNT_CONTROL	= LOAD
190	MY_PIPELINE_ENABLE	= '0'
190	MY_Y_CONTROL	= SELECT_UPC
190	MY_STACK_CONTROL	= S_NOOP
190	MY_UPC_CONTROL	= COUNT
190	MY_INTERRUPT_VECTOR_ENABLE	= '1'
190	MY_MAPPING_ROM_ENABLE	= '1'

200 NS

200	MY_INSTRUCTION	= LOP
200	MY_STACK_CONTROL	= S_POP
200	MY_PIPELINE_ENABLE	= '0'
200	MY_REGCNT_CONTROL	= LOAD
200	MY_Y_CONTROL	= SELECT_UPC
200	MY_UPC_CONTROL	= COUNT
200	MY_INTERRUPT_VECTOR_ENABLE	= '1'
200	MY_MAPPING_ROM_ENABLE	= '1'

210 NS

210	MY_INSTRUCTION	= CONT
210	MY_PIPELINE_ENABLE	= '0'
210	MY_REGCNT_CONTROL	= LOAD
210	MY_Y_CONTROL	= SELECT_UPC
210	MY_STACK_CONTROL	= S_NOOP
210	MY_UPC_CONTROL	= COUNT
210	MY_INTERRUPT_VECTOR_ENABLE	= '1'
210	MY_MAPPING_ROM_ENABLE	= '1'

220 NS

220	MY_INSTRUCTION	= TWB
220	MY_STACK_CONTROL	= S_POP
220	MY_PIPELINE_ENABLE	= '0'
220	MY_REGCNT_CONTROL	= LOAD

220	MY_Y_CONTROL	= SELECT_UPC
220	MY_UPC_CONTROL	= COUNT
220	MY_INTERRUPT_VECTOR_ENABLE	= '1'
220	MY_MAPPING_ROM_ENABLE	= '1'

Stack.vhd

The stack module is a simple LIFO stack network with push, pop, clear and no-operation instructions. It will hold up to nine of the 2910 12-bit addresses, and has a overflow detection output. The registers of the stack are composed of register three-state buffer combinations; each element of the stack has its out-put tied together as a three-state bus configuration. This requires the use of a bus resolution function for simulation that will be ignored by the logic synthesis system (the synthesis tool will wire all of the drivers together). Because the stack module contains a regular array of storage elements, we can use some of the structural elements of VHDL to cut down on the description task.

First is a description of the basic storage location type used for each word of the stack. This submodule is called STACK_ELEMENT. This module registers its inputs on a rising gated (by the write enable signal) clock edge by using the wait statement, while the outputs of the register are tied to an array of three-state buffers. Note that a design decision is made to use the negative data sense coming into the stack, so that an inverting three-state buffer is required at the stack output. An enable input to each STACK_ELEMENT is provided that will activate the three-state output of a particular storage word.

```
-- One 12-bit element of the stack.
-- A 12-bit flip-flop with tri-state output.
--
use work.SYNOPSYS.all;
use work.AMD_PACK.all;

entity STACK_ELEMENT is
 port( VALUE: in ADDRESS ;
        CLOCK: in BIT ;
        WRITE_ENABLE: in BIT ;
        OUTPUT_ENABLE: in BIT ;
        OUTPUT: out ADDRESS) ;
end STACK_ELEMENT ;

use work.SYNOPSYS.all ;
use work.AMD_PACK.all ;

architecture STACK_ELEMENT_HDL of
STACK_ELEMENT is
 -- Three-state element from target library
 component BTS5
   port(A: in BIT; E: in BIT; z: out BIT) ;
 end component ;
 signal GATED_CLOCK: BIT ;
 signal LATCHED_VALUE : ADDRESS;

begin
 -- make gated clock for flip-flop
 GATED_CLOCK <= CLOCK and WRITE_ENABLE ;
 -- make flip-flop
 process
 begin
   wait until (not GATED_CLOCK'stable and
           GATED_CLOCK = '1') ;
  LATCHED_VALUE <= VALUE;
 end process ;
```

```
-- Three-state the output (use three-state from library)
U1: BTS5 port map(LATCHED_VALUE(1),
    OUTPUT_ENABLE, OUTPUT(1));
U2: BTS5 port map(LATCHED_VALUE(2),
    OUTPUT_ENABLE, OUTPUT(2));
U3: BTS5 port map(LATCHED_VALUE(3),
    OUTPUT_ENABLE, OUTPUT(3));
U4: BTS5 port map(LATCHED_VALUE(4),
    OUTPUT_ENABLE, OUTPUT(4));
U5: BTS5 port map(LATCHED_VALUE(5),
    OUTPUT_ENABLE, OUTPUT(5));
U6: BTS5 port map(LATCHED_VALUE(6),
    OUTPUT_ENABLE, OUTPUT(6));
U7: BTS5 port map(LATCHED_VALUE(7),
    OUTPUT_ENABLE, OUTPUT(7));
U8: BTS5 port map(LATCHED_VALUE(8),
    OUTPUT_ENABLE, OUTPUT(8));
U9: BTS5 port map(LATCHED_VALUE(9),
    OUTPUT_ENABLE, OUTPUT(9));
U10: BTS5 port
    map(LATCHED_VALUE(10),OUTPUT_ENABLE,
    OUTPUT(10));
U11: BTS5 port
    map(LATCHED_VALUE(11),OUTPUT_ENABLE,
    OUTPUT(11));
U12: BTS5 port
    map(LATCHED_VALUE(12),OUTPUT_ENABLE,
    OUTPUT(12));

end STACK_ELEMENT_HDL ;
```

Using the storage elements of STACK_ELEMENTs as basic building blocks, the top level description of STACK now needs only to instantiate the array of memory required, and provide the read and write control mechanism to get the FIFO stack behavior desired.

The basic idea with the control logic for this module is to have both a push and a read pointer (output enable) to determine where to write to next, and which word to be considered as the stack top. The control is broken into two processes. One process to register the stack pointers, so that the current location is maintained between clock cycles, and the other describes the combinational control of the next stack pointer values, and the read and write enable lines (these values are allowed to change on other than clock boundaries).

```
--      Run-time stack module
--
--      Maintains a stack of nine 12-bit addresses.
--      Its 4 operations are:
--
--      S_NOOP:  Do nothing
--      S_CLEAR: Flush the stack
--      S_POP:   Move the stack pointer back
--      S_PUSH:  Write the given "VALUE" and
--      move up the stack pointer.
```

```
-- "OUTPUT_VALUE" always is value at the top of
-- the stack.
-- "OVERFLOW" will be set when the stack is full.
--
use work.SYNOPSYS.all;
use work.AMD_PACK.all;

entity STACK is
  port(OPERATION    : in STACK_OPS;
       VALUE        : in ADDRESS;
       CLOCK        : in BIT;
       OUTPUT_VALUE : out wired_or ADDRESS;
       OVERFLOW : out BIT);
end STACK;
```

Output port with bus resolution function

```
architecture STACK_HDL of STACK is
-- Three-state latch used to store stack element data
  component STACK_ELEMENT
    port(VALUE: in ADDRESS; CLOCK: in BIT;
         WRITE_ENABLE: in BIT;
         OUTPUT_ENABLE: in BIT; OUTPUT: out
            ADDRESS);
  end component;

  signal WRITE_ENABLE  : STACK_VECTOR;
  signal READ_ENABLE   : STACK_VECTOR;
  signal STK_PTR       : STACK_VECTOR_SIZE;
-- read ptr
  signal PSH_PTR       : STACK_VECTOR_SIZE;
-- next write
  signal NEXT_STK      : STACK_VECTOR_SIZE;
  signal NEXT_PSH      : STACK_VECTOR_SIZE;
```

```
begin

  -- process to compute next stack ptrs and
  -- read/write enable
  STACK_LOGIC : process(clock,operation,value)
```

Enables writing during PUSH operation

```
begin
    WRITE_ENABLE <= STACK_VECTOR'(others => '0');
    if (OPERATION = S_PUSH) then
        WRITE_ENABLE(PSH_PTR) <= '1' ;
    end if;
```

Enables reading from top of stack

```
    READ_ENABLE <= STACK_VECTOR'(others => '0');
    READ_ENABLE(STK_PTR) <= '1';
```

Calculates new value for stack top pointer

```
    if (OPERATION = S_NOOP) then
        NEXT_STK <= STK_PTR;
        NEXT_PSH <= PSH_PTR;
        OVERFLOW <= '0';

    elsif (OPERATION = S_CLEAR) then
        NEXT_STK <= STACK_VECTOR'LOW;
        NEXT_PSH <= STACK_VECTOR'LOW;
        OVERFLOW <= '0';

    elsif (OPERATION = S_PUSH)  then
```

```
        if (PSH_PTR < STACK_VECTOR'HIGH) then          U2: STACK_ELEMENT port map(VALUE, CLOCK,
          NEXT_PSH <= PSH_PTR + 1;                        WRITE_ENABLE(2),
         OVERFLOW <= '0';                                      READ_ENABLE(2), OUTPUT_VALUE);
        else                                            U3: STACK_ELEMENT port map(VALUE, CLOCK,
         OVERFLOW <= '1';                                  WRITE_ENABLE(3),
        end if;                                               READ_ENABLE(3), OUTPUT_VALUE);
        NEXT_STK <= PSH_PTR;                            U4: STACK_ELEMENT port map(VALUE, CLOCK,
                                                           WRITE_ENABLE(4),
    elsif (OPERATION = S_POP)   then                          READ_ENABLE(4), OUTPUT_VALUE);
        if (PSH_PTR > STACK_VECTOR'LOW) and            U5: STACK_ELEMENT port map(VALUE, CLOCK,
          (PSH_PTR /= STK_PTR) then                       WRITE_ENABLE(5),
            NEXT_PSH <= PSH_PTR - 1;                          READ_ENABLE(5), OUTPUT_VALUE);
        end if;                                         U6: STACK_ELEMENT port map(VALUE, CLOCK,
        if (STK_PTR > STACK_VECTOR'LOW) then              WRITE_ENABLE(6),
         NEXT_STK <= STK_PTR - 1;                             READ_ENABLE(6), OUTPUT_VALUE);
        end if;                                         U7: STACK_ELEMENT port map(VALUE, CLOCK,
        OVERFLOW <= '0';                                   WRITE_ENABLE(7),
    end if;                                                   READ_ENABLE(7), OUTPUT_VALUE);
                                                        U8: STACK_ELEMENT port map(VALUE, CLOCK,
                                                           WRITE_ENABLE(8),
end process STACK_LOGIC;                                      READ_ENABLE(8), OUTPUT_VALUE);
                                                        U9: STACK_ELEMENT port map(VALUE, CLOCK,
                                                           WRITE_ENABLE(9),
STK_REG_GEN : process                                        READ_ENABLE(9), OUTPUT_VALUE);
begin
 wait until not clock' stable  and  clock = '1';
 STK_PTR <= NEXT_STK;
 PSH_PTR <= NEXT_PSH;
end process STK_REG_GEN;                          end STACK_HDL;
```

Registers here store stack top pointer

Stack is 9 deep.

```
-- Stack values, controlled by read and write enables set
-- above
 U1: STACK_ELEMENT port map(VALUE, CLOCK,
     WRITE_ENABLE(1),
      READ_ENABLE(1), OUTPUT_VALUE);
```

The simulation of the stack performs a random set of PUSH, POP, and CLEAR operations. Following are the results of the simulation.

40 OPERATION   = S_NOOP
  INPUT VALUE = X"000"
  OUTPUT VALUE = X"FFF" (X"000")
  OVERFLOW   = '0'

80 OPERATION = S_PUSH
  INPUT VALUE = X"C00"
  OUTPUT VALUE = X"3FF" (X"C00")
  OVERFLOW   = '0'

120 OPERATION = S_PUSH
  INPUT VALUE = X"800"
  OUTPUT VALUE = X"7FF" (X"800")
  OVERFLOW   = '0'

160 OPERATION = S_PUSH
  INPUT VALUE = X"C00"
  OUTPUT VALUE = X"3FF" (X"C00")
  OVERFLOW   = '0'

200 OPERATION = S_NOOP
  INPUT VALUE = X"000"
  OUTPUT VALUE = X"3FF" (X"C00")
  OVERFLOW   = '0'

240 OPERATION = S_POP
  INPUT VALUE = X"000"
  OUTPUT VALUE = X"7FF" (X"800")
  OVERFLOW   = '0'

280 OPERATION = S_POP
  INPUT VALUE = X"000"
  OUTPUT VALUE = X"3FF" (X"C00")
  OVERFLOW   = '0'

320 OPERATION = S_POP
  INPUT VALUE = X"000"
  OUTPUT VALUE = X"3FF" (X"C00")
  OVERFLOW   = '0'

360 OPERATION = S_PUSH
  INPUT VALUE = X"001"
  OUTPUT VALUE = X"FFE" (X"001")
  OVERFLOW   = '0'

400 OPERATION   = S_PUSH
  INPUT VALUE = X"002"
  OUTPUT VALUE = X"FFD" (X"002")
  OVERFLOW   = '0'

440 OPERATION   = S_CLEAR
  INPUT VALUE = X"000"
  OUTPUT VALUE = X"FFE" (X"001")
  OVERFLOW   = '0'

Simulating the Am2910

Now that each of the major functional modules is created and validated, the system as a whole can be tested. The top level module of the 2910 consists of signal declarations used for interconnection, and the instantiation of the five functional blocks created.

```
use work.SYNOPSYS.all;
use work.AMD_PACK.all;
```

```
Declare ports at top level
```

```
entity AM2910 is
  port(D                    : in ADDRESS;
       INSTRUCTION    : in INSTRUCTION_OPS;
       CONDITION_CODE           : in BIT;
       CONDITION_CODE_ENABLE : in BIT;
       CARRY_IN      : in BIT;
       RELOAD        : in BIT;
       ENABLE_Y      : in BIT;
       CLOCK         : in BIT;
       Y_OUTPUT      : buffer ADDRESS;
       OVERFLOW      : out BIT;
       PIPELINE_ENABLE          : out BIT;
       MAPPING_ROM_ENABLE       : out BIT;
       INTERRUPT_DRIVER_ENABLE: out BIT);
  end AM2910;
```

```
Declare five major sub-blocks
```

```
architecture HDL of AM2910 is
  component CONTROL
    port(INSTRUCTION: in INSTRUCTION_OPS;
         CONDITION_CODE      : in BIT;
         CONDITION_CODE_ENABLE    : in BIT;
```

```
         FORCE_LOAD : in BIT;
         REGCNT_ZERO : in BIT;
         UPC_CONTROL: out UPC_OPS;
         STACK_CONTROL : out STACK_OPS;
         REGCNT_CONTROL : out REGCNT_OPS;
         Y_CONTROL : out Y_MUX_OPS;
         PIPELINE_ENABLE  : out BIT;
         MAPPING_ROM_ENABLE : out BIT;
         INTERRUPT_VECTOR_ENABLE : out BIT);
  end component;
```

```
  component REGCNT
    port(OPERATION : in REGCNT_OPS;
         DATA : in ADDRESS;
         CLOCK : in BIT;
         OUTPUT : buffer ADDRESS;
         ZERO: out BIT);
  end component;
```

```
  component STACK
    port(OPERATION : in STACK_OPS;
         VALUE : in ADDRESS;
         CLOCK : in BIT;
         OUTPUT_VALUE : out ADDRESS;
         OVERFLOW : out BIT);
  end component;
```

```
  component UPC
    port(OPERATION: in UPC_OPS;
         DATA : in ADDRESS;
         CARRY_IN : in BIT;
         CLOCK : in BIT;
         OUTPUT : buffer ADDRESS;
         OUTPUT_BAR : out ADDRESS);
  end component;
```

```vhdl
component Y
  port(OPERATION      : in Y_MUX_OPS;
       DATA_IN        : in ADDRESS;
       REGCNT_IN      : in ADDRESS;
       STACK_IN       : in ADDRESS;
       UPC_IN: in ADDRESS;
       MUXOUT         : out ADDRESS);
end component;

-- Top-level nets that connect major submodules
signal REGCNT_OP : REGCNT_OPS;
-- Register/counter control signal
 signal STACK_OP  : STACK_OPS;
-- Stack control signal
 signal UPC_OP    : UPC_OPS;
-- UPC control signal
 signal Y_OP      : Y_MUX_OPS;
-- Mux control signal

 signal REGCNT_OUT  : ADDRESS;
-- Register/count output
 signal REGCNT_ZERO : BIT;
-- Register/counter zero flag
 signal STACK_TOP   : ADDRESS;
-- Top of the stack
 signal UPC_OUT     : ADDRESS;
-- UPC output
 signal UPC_OUT_BAR : ADDRESS;
-- UPC output inverted
 signal TMP_Y_OUTPUT: ADDRESS;
```

┌───┐
│ **Structural VHDL for top-level netlist** │
└───┘

```vhdl
begin
-- Instantiate the five functional units
```

```vhdl
 U1: STACK port map(STACK_OP, UPC_OUT_BAR,
    CLOCK, STACK_TOP, OVERFLOW);

 U2: UPC port map(UPC_OP, Y_OUTPUT,
    CARRY_IN, CLOCK, UPC_OUT, UPC_OUT_BAR);

 U3: REGCNT port map(REGCNT_OP, D, CLOCK,
    REGCNT_OUT, REGCNT_ZERO);

 U4: Y port map(Y_OP, D, REGCNT_OUT,
    STACK_TOP, UPC_OUT, TMP_Y_OUTPUT);

Y_OUTPUT <= TMP_Y_OUTPUT;

 U5: CONTROL port map(INSTRUCTION,
    CONDITION_CODE,
    CONDITION_CODE_ENABLE, RELOAD,
    REGCNT_ZERO,
    UPC_OP, STACK_OP, REGCNT_OP, Y_OP,
    PIPELINE_ENABLE, MAPPING_ROM_ENABLE,
    INTERRUPT_DRIVER_ENABLE);
end HDL;
```

To validate the functional behavior of the overall design, a slightly different approach is taken than was used for the individual modules. A small, self contained microcontroller system is constructed to stimulate and test the response of the 2910. The system contains a pipeline register and a read-only memory along with the 2910. The ROM is loaded with a program for the 2910 to execute. If all goes well, then, a fixed sequence of instructions will be executed from the ROM; if there are any execution errors, the sequence of

fers from the execution desired path. Following is the architecture. The portion of the test driver containing the test program is included below. The ROM was modeled as an array of ADDRESS's. Signal assignments are used to set the contents of each relevant memory location, and a small

process with a 100 ns wait statement generates the clock signal for the system.

```
-- nop's
        MEM(0) <= '0' & X"ce000";
        MEM(1) <= '0' & X"ce001";
        MEM(2) <= '0' & X"ce002";
```

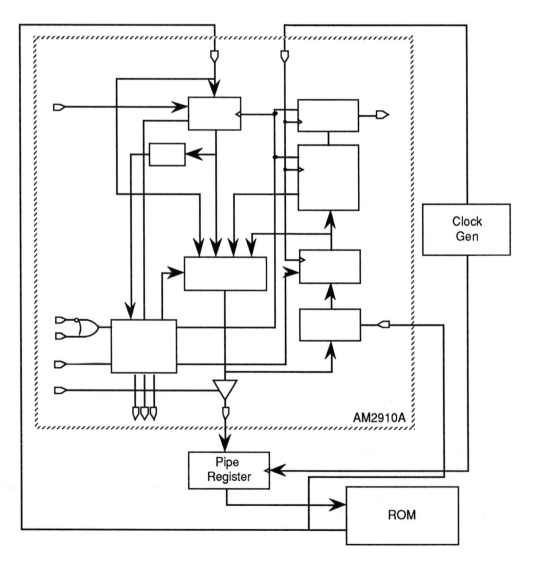

```
        MEM(3) <= '0' & X"ce003";
        MEM(4) <= '0' & X"d10ff";
-- don't jump to sub at 20
        MEM(5) <= '0' & X"c1020";
-- now jmp
-- let's check out the full flag - fill the stack
        MEM(6) <= '0' & X"d4006";
        MEM(7) <= '0' & X"d4007";
        MEM(8) <= '0' & X"d4008";
        MEM(9) <= '0' & X"d4009";

        MEM(10) <= '0' & X"d400a";
        MEM(11) <= '0' & X"d400b";
        MEM(12) <= '0' & X"d400c";
        MEM(13) <= '0' & X"d400d";
        MEM(14) <= '0' & X"d400e";

-- we'll even go so far as to fill it too much
        MEM(15) <= '0' & X"d400f";

-- and empty the stack
        MEM(16) <= '0' & X"cd010";
        MEM(17) <= '0' & X"cd011";
        MEM(18) <= '0' & X"cd012";
        MEM(19) <= '0' & X"cd013";
        MEM(20) <= '0' & X"cd014";

        MEM(21) <= '0' & X"cd015";
        MEM(22) <= '0' & X"cd016";
        MEM(23) <= '0' & X"cd017";
        MEM(24) <= '0' & X"cd018";

-- again, too much
        MEM(25) <= '0' & X"cd019";
        MEM(26) <= '0' & X"c1028";
-- now jsr to 28
        MEM(27) <= '0' & X"8efff";
```

```
-- hold here
-- @020
        MEM(32) <= '0' & X"d4020";
-- don't load the counter
        MEM(33) <= '0' & X"cd021";
-- but clean the stack
        MEM(34) <= '0' & X"c4008";
-- load the counter
        MEM(35) <= '0' & X"c8022";
-- loop for a while
        MEM(36) <= '0' & X"da024";
-- don't return from this subroutine
        MEM(37) <= '0' & X"ca025";
-- return from this subroutine
-- @028
        MEM(40) <= '0' & X"c202c";
-- Now lets try JMAP
        MEM(41) <= '0' & X"8ebad";
-- If we get here we're messed up
-- @02c
        MEM(44) <= '0' & X"d30ff";
-- going on, lets try a CJP
-- first don't jump
        MEM(45) <= '0' & X"c3030";
-- going on, lets try a CJP - now jump
-- @030
MEM(48) <= '0' & X"c40ff";
-- load the counter with 0ff
        MEM(49) <= '0' & X"cd031";
-- pop the extra word off the stack
        MEM(50) <= '0' & X"cc0ff";
-- load the counter with 0ff
        MEM(51) <= '0' & X"c50fe";
-- test the jsr
        MEM(52) <= '0' & X"4e0fe";
-- load the counter directly
        MEM(53) <= '0' & X"d50ff";
```

-- try the jsr from the counter
        MEM(54) <= '0' & X"d60ff";
-- Try the conditional jump (fail)
        MEM(55) <= '0' & X"c603c";
-- do a conditional jump
        MEM(56) <= '0' & X"8ebad";
-- shouldn't get here
-- @03c
        MEM(60) <= '0' & X"cc0ff";
-- load the counter with 0ff
        MEM(61) <= '0' & X"c7040";
-- jump to the counter contents
        MEM(62) <= '0' & X"8ebad";
-- @040
        MEM(64) <= '0' & X"cc044";
-- jumping via counter to 044
        MEM(65) <= '0' & X"d70ff";
-- jump via counter
        MEM(66) <= '0' & X"8ebad";
-- @044
        MEM(68) <= '0' & X"cc004";
-- gonna loop 4 times
        MEM(69) <= '0' & X"d9045";
-- loop back 4 times
        MEM(70) <= '0' & X"cc001";
-- use this loop to jump via d
        MEM(71) <= '0' & X"c904c";
-- jump to 04c
        MEM(72) <= '0' & X"8ebad";
-- @04c
        MEM(76) <= '0' & X"c40ff";
-- push a bad address
        MEM(77) <= '0' & X"db0ff";
-- fail this conditional jump
        MEM(78) <= '0' & X"cb054";
-- go to 054
        MEM(79) <= '0' & X"8ebad";

-- @054
        MEM(84) <= '0' & X"c40ff";
-- push address
        MEM(85) <= '0' & X"cf0ff";
-- pop the address and continue
        MEM(86) <= '0' & X"c40ff";
-- push address
        MEM(87) <= '0' & X"cc000";
-- clear the counter
        MEM(88) <= '0' & X"df05c";
-- jump to 05c
        MEM(89) <= '0' & X"8ebad";
-- @05c

        MEM(92) <= '0' & X"c4004";
-- load a count and push next
        MEM(93) <= '0' & X"df060";
-- jump to 060
        MEM(94) <= '0' & X"8ebad";
-- @060
        MEM(96) <= '0' & X"8aaaa";
-- good return
-- @0fe
        MEM(254) <= '0' & X"ca0fe";
-- This is where most jsr's go
        MEM(255) <= '0' & X"8ebad";
-- This is where all (most) bad
--   instructions end up

The above program is written so that if execution proceeds correctly, then execution ends at ROM location 27. Because the simulation listing is lengthy, only an abbreviated listing is included.

Examining the execution path in the simulation results reveals that the functional behavior described is indeed that of the AM2910A. At this point the system description is completed, validated, and is now ready to be sent through the synthesis process.

0 CONTROL_PORTS:
    instruction = JMAP ((cc,cce)=('1','1'))
    force_load = '1' regcnt_zero = '1'
    upc_control = COUNT
    stack_control = S_NOOP
    regcnt_control= NOOP
    y_control = SELECT_DATA
    NEXT_ROM_ADDR = 0 Y_OUTPUT = X"000"

100 CONTROL_PORTS:
    instruction = JMAP ((cc,cce)=('1','1'))
    force_load = '1' regcnt_zero = '1'
    upc_control = COUNT stack_control = S_NOOP
    regcnt_control= NOOP
    y_control = SELECT_DATA
    NEXT_ROM_ADDR = 0 Y_OUTPUT = X"000"

200 CONTROL_PORTS:
    instruction = JZ ((cc,cce)=('0','0'))
    force_load = '0' regcnt_zero = '1'
    upc_control = CLEAR stack_control = S_CLEAR
    regcnt_control= LOAD
    y_control = SELECT_NONE
    NEXT_ROM_ADDR = 0 Y_OUTPUT = X"000"

300 CONTROL_PORTS:
    instruction = JZ ((cc,cce)=('0','0'))
    force_load = '0' regcnt_zero = '1'

upc_control = CLEAR stack_control = S_CLEAR
regcnt_control = LOAD
y_control = SELECT_NONE
NEXT_ROM_ADDR = 0 Y_OUTPUT = X"000"

400 CONTROL_PORTS:
    instruction = CONT ((cc,cce)=('0','0'))
    force_load = '1' regcnt_zero = '1'
    upc_control = COUNT stack_control = S_NOOP
    regcnt_control= NOOP y_control = SELECT_UPC
    NEXT_ROM_ADDR = 0 Y_OUTPUT = X"000"

500 CONTROL_PORTS:
    instruction = CONT ((cc,cce)=('0','0'))
    force_load = '1' regcnt_zero = '1'
    upc_control = COUNT stack_control = S_NOOP
    regcnt_control= NOOP y_control = SELECT_UPC
    NEXT_ROM_ADDR = 0 Y_OUTPUT = X"001"

600 CONTROL_PORTS:
    instruction = CONT ((cc,cce)=('0','0'))
    force_load = '1' regcnt_zero = '1'
    upc_control = COUNT stack_control = S_NOOP
    regcnt_control= NOOP y_control = SELECT_UPC
    NEXT_ROM_ADDR = 1 Y_OUTPUT = X"001"

700 CONTROL_PORTS:
    instruction = CONT ((cc,cce)=('0','0'))
    force_load = '1' regcnt_zero = '1'
    upc_control = COUNT stack_control = S_NOOP
    regcnt_control= NOOP y_control = SELECT_UPC
    NEXT_ROM_ADDR = 1 Y_OUTPUT = X"002"

800 CONTROL_PORTS:
    instruction = CONT ((cc,cce)=('0','0'))
    force_load = '1' regcnt_zero = '1'

```
        upc_control  = COUNT  stack_control = S_NOOP
        regcnt_control= NOOP  y_control  = SELECT_UPC
        NEXT_ROM_ADDR = 2  Y_OUTPUT    = X"002"


 900 CONTROL_PORTS:
        instruction  = CONT   ((cc,cce)=('0','0'))
        force_load   = '1'          regcnt_zero = '1'
        upc_control  = COUNT  stack_control = S_NOOP
        regcnt_control= NOOP  y_control  = SELECT_UPC
        NEXT_ROM_ADDR = 2  Y_OUTPUT    = X"003"


1000 CONTROL_PORTS:
        instruction  = CONT   ((cc,cce)=('0','0'))
        force_load   = '1'          regcnt_zero = '1'
        upc_control  = COUNT  stack_control = S_NOOP
        regcnt_control= NOOP  y_control  = SELECT_UPC
        NEXT_ROM_ADDR = 3  Y_OUTPUT    = X"003"


1100 CONTROL_PORTS:
        instruction  = CONT   ((cc,cce)=('0','0'))
        force_load   = '1'          regcnt_zero = '1'
        upc_control  = COUNT  stack_control = S_NOOP
        regcnt_control= NOOP  y_control  = SELECT_UPC
        NEXT_ROM_ADDR = 3  Y_OUTPUT    = X"004"


1200 CONTROL_PORTS:
        instruction  = CONT   ((cc,cce)=('0','0'))
        force_load   = '1'  regcnt_zero = '1'
        upc_control  = COUNT  stack_control = S_NOOP
        regcnt_control= NOOP  y_control  = SELECT_UPC
        NEXT_ROM_ADDR = 4  Y_OUTPUT    = X"004"
1300 CONTROL_PORTS:
        instruction  = CONT   ((cc,cce)=('0','0'))
        force_load   = '1'          regcnt_zero = '1'
        upc_control  = COUNT  stack_control = S_NOOP
        regcnt_control= NOOP  y_control  = SELECT_UPC
        NEXT_ROM_ADDR = 4  Y_OUTPUT    = X"005"


1400 CONTROL_PORTS:
        instruction  = CJS  ((cc,cce)=('1','0'))
        force_load   = '1'   regcnt_zero = '1'
        upc_control  = COUNT  stack_control = S_NOOP
        regcnt_control= NOOP  y_control  = SELECT_UPC
        NEXT_ROM_ADDR = 5  Y_OUTPUT    = X"005"


1500 CONTROL_PORTS:
        instruction  = CJS  ((cc,cce)=('1','0'))
        force_load   = '1'          regcnt_zero  = '1'
        upc_control  = COUNT  stack_control = S_NOOP
        regcnt_control= NOOP  y_control  = SELECT_UPC
        NEXT_ROM_ADDR = 5  Y_OUTPUT    = X"006"


1600 CONTROL_PORTS:
        instruction  = CJS  ((cc,cce)=('0','0'))
        force_load   = '1'  regcnt_zero  = '1'
        upc_control  = COUNT  stack_control = S_PUSH
        regcnt_control= NOOP  y_control  = SELECT_DATA
        NEXT_ROM_ADDR = 32  Y_OUTPUT     = X"020"


1700 CONTROL_PORTS:
        instruction  = CJS  ((cc,cce)=('0','0'))
        force_load   = '1'  regcnt_zero  = '1'
        upc_control  = COUNT  stack_control = S_PUSH
        regcnt_control= NOOP  y_control  = SELECT_DATA
        NEXT_ROM_ADDR = 32  Y_OUTPUT    = X"020"


1800 CONTROL_PORTS:
        instruction  = PUSH  ((cc,cce)=('1','0'))
        force_load   = '1'          regcnt_zero  = '1'
        upc_control  = COUNT  stack_control = S_PUSH
        regcnt_control= NOOP  y_control  = SELECT_UPC
        NEXT_ROM_ADDR = 33  Y_OUTPUT    = X"021"
```

1900 CONTROL_PORTS:

     instruction = PUSH ((cc,cce)=('1','0'))
     force_load = '1'   regcnt_zero = '1'
     upc_control = COUNT stack_control = S_PUSH
     regcnt_control= NOOP y_control = SELECT_UPC
     NEXT_ROM_ADDR = 33 Y_OUTPUT   = X"022"

2000 CONTROL_PORTS:

     instruction = LOP ((cc,cce)=('0','0'))
     force_load = '1'   regcnt_zero = '1'
     upc_control = COUNT stack_control = S_POP
     regcnt_control= NOOP y_control = SELECT_UPC
     NEXT_ROM_ADDR = 34 Y_OUTPUT   = X"022"

Synthesis of the AM2910

The previous sections of Chapter 6 have focused on the functional design of the AM2910A. In the following sections, the AM2910A RTL description developed is transformed into an optimized gate-level design via automated synthesis technology.

The synthesis process is carried out in much the same manner as the development of the RTL model; the design will be processed one functional unit at a time. This approach has two major benefits: 1) the design hierarchy is maintained (this may be desirable for layout or other considerations), 2) a different optimization strategy can be used for each piece of the design.

The main drawback of this approach is that optimization across functional unit boundaries is prevented; it is usually possible to get further optimization improvements by collapsing the entire design hierarchy into a single level. However, the added optimization benefits must be weighed against the value of maintaining the hierarchy. In this document, we also include optimization of the entire design as a single module.

The Synopsys Design Compiler and the VHDL option of the HDL Complier are used in concert to perform the gate-level synthesis of the 2910. Complete information on all of the tool options and features is available in the tool reference manual. Here, we will only outline the process.

To complete the design of the 2910, and the subsequent documentation of the process, an eight step procedure was followed for each module. The procedure used typifies the use of synthesis tools for large designs (10 to 30 times the size of the 2910). Each step in the process is listed with its input, output, and purpose.

The results reported for the synthesis process are from the first beta release of the VHDL option of the HDL Compiler. Algorithmic improvements, and optimization strategy changes are made regularly to enhance the quality of results. For this reason, the actual results will vary from release to release.

1. Read the VHDL RTL source. The VHDL files must be processed in VHDL Language Reference Manual (LRM) prescribed order. The read command performs the syntax and semantic checking on the source file(s), and produces a control flow/data flow data structure for the HDL framework of the HDL Complier. The HDL Compiler then translates the design into a boolean logic level representation, ready for mapping and optimization by the Design Compiler. Below is an example of reading all of the modules simultaneously:

```
read -f vhdl { synopsys.vhd amd_pack.vhd stack.vhd \
   regcnt.vhd upc.vhd y.vhd control.vhd am2910.vhd }
```

2. Map each module into gates.

For this experiment, a commercial 1.5 micron CMOS sea of gates library will be used. The idea is to quickly get each module of the design mapped into the gates of the target technology. We wish to maintain the design hierarchy (for now anyway), so each module is mapped individually by switching the current design context, and compiling into gates. This quick mapping into gates allows the computation of module interface parameters that are helpful during optimization. Below the commands used to map each module of the 2910 are shown:

```
current_design = Y;            compile
current_design = UPC;          compile
current_design = REGCNT;       compile
current_design = CONTROL;      compile
current_design = STACK;        compile
```

3. Set interface & environment parameters.

This step computes the effects of module interaction, and the external environment. Each module needs loading information at each of its output ports, arrival times and drive strengths of signals at its input ports. The design as a whole also needs such external interface information, as well as operating condition, and wire loading information. The commands shown below outline how such information is computed:

```
current_design = AM2910;
/* top level design
*/ set_drive 0.02 all_inputs();
/* drive into 2910
*/ set_load 2 all_outputs();
 /* load on outputs of 2910
*/ set_operating_conditions ("WCCOM");
 /* operating range
*/ set_wire_load ("10x10");
 /* interconnect estimation
*/current_design = AM2910;
/* move to top level module
*/characterize U1;
 /* compute arrival times. loads, etc. */
```

4. Set constraints.

Now the design goals for each module are set so that the optimizer knows what it is aiming for. The tool uses a sophisticated combination of algorithmic and rule-based techniques to perform optimizations and speed-area trade-offs in both the boolean and gate domains. Setting speed and area goals for the design tells the tools how to make these trade-offs. Because the modules have already been mapped to gates, a preliminary report on the size and speed of each module can be obtained as a starting point for deciding on the design goals. Below, the three sets of design constraints used for the synthesis of the REGCNT module are shown:

```
/* Area only optimization */
current_design = REGCNT;
max_area 0;

/* Speed only optimization */
current_design = REGCNT;
max_delay 0 all_outputs();
clocks_at 0 0 0  CLOCK;

/* Speed/Area trade-off optimization */
current_design = REGCNT;
max_area 200;
clocks_at 0 0 11.0  CLOCK;
max_delay 3.0  all_outputs();
```

5. Optimize. Once the designs are read into the system, and have all of their interface, environment, and design goals set they can be optimized. There are a number of different optimization strategies that can be employed that take advantage of different optimization techniques. Refer to the Design Compiler Reference Manual for complete details. For the 2910, only the default optimization settings were used. After setup the compile command is used to perform the technology specific optimization:

```
current_design = REGCNT;
compile;
```

6. Generate schematics. For design documentation purpose, it is often a requirement to have a gate-level design schematic. For thepurposes of this document, it is illustrative to use the schematics to visualize the speed area trade-offs made by Design Compiler. Two commands are used to generate, and then plot the schematic of a design:

```
gen;  /* generate a schematic for 'view' or 'plot' */
plot;  /* send schematic to a postscript plotter   */
```

7. Write out the design. The resulting design can be saved in a number of different formats (EDIF 2.0, TDL, MIF, etc.). For the 2910 we have chosen to write out a VHDL structural model using the write command:

```
write -f vhdl -o AREA_OPT.vhd
```

8. Report the results. The final design statistics are also useful information for design documentation. Design Compiler has the capability to report on a whole host of design properties and statistics. Refer to the Design Compiler Reference Manual for complete details. For this document we are concerned with area, speed, and how the optimizer performed with respect to our specific design goals. The report commands below show how to obtain this information and save it into a file:

```
report -area -timing > AREA_OPT.rpt
report -constraint   > AREA_OPT.cstr_rpt
```

The synthesis of each module of the 2910 follows, each module in its own section. The procedure outlined above was used on each module to arrive at the reported results. The entire 2910 is then examined to report on the results of the HDL design methodology we have employed.

Synthesis of the Y Module

The Y module (multiplexer) is made up of purely combinational logic. This sub-module encompasses approximately 155 gate equivalents when mapped without design constraints to the 1.5 micron CMOS library.

The first optimization was the area-only optimization. The timing and area report is shown below:

Information: Updating design information. (UID-85)

```
*****************************************
Report : area
Design : Y
Version: 1.2-beta2
Date   : Mon Sep  4 20:10:00 1989
*****************************************
```

Library(s) Used:
    CMOS_1.5 (File: /osi7/release/v1.2-beta2/libraries/
CMOS_1.5.db)

Number of ports:	63
Number of nets:	95
Number of cells:	44
Number of references:	5

Combinational area:	69.00	
Noncombinational area:	0.00	
Net Interconnect area:	0.00	(No wire load specified)

Total area: 69.00

```
*****************************************
Report : timing
   -path end
   -delay max
Design : Y
Version: 1.2-beta2
Date   : Mon Sep  4 20:10:00 1989
*****************************************
```

Operating Conditions:
Wire Loading Model:

Point	Type	Fanout	Max Delay rise	fall	Min Delay rise	fall
MUXOUT_1	output	1	5.68	3.25	1.05	1.21
MUXOUT_2	output	1	5.68	3.25	1.05	1.21
MUXOUT_3	output	1	5.68	3.25	1.05	1.21
MUXOUT_4	output	1	5.68	3.25	1.05	1.21
MUXOUT_5	output	1	5.68	3.25	1.05	1.21
MUXOUT_6	output	1	5.68	3.25	1.05	1.21
MUXOUT_7	output	1	5.68	3.25	1.05	1.21
MUXOUT_8	output	1	5.68	3.25	1.05	1.21
MUXOUT_9	output	1	5.68	3.25	1.05	1.21
MUXOUT_10	output	1	5.68	3.25	1.05	1.21
MUXOUT_11	output	1	5.68	3.25	1.05	1.21
MUXOUT_12	output	1	5.68	3.25	1.05	1.21

As shown, the critical path delay is 5.68 nS, while the design area is only 69 gate equivalents.

Next we perform the "speed-only" optimization on the Y module to get the following results:

Information: Updating design information. (UID-85)

Library(s) Used:

    CMOS_1.5 (File: /osi7/release/v1.2-beta2/libraries/
CMOS_1.5.db)

Point	Type	Fanout	Max Delay rise	fall	Min Delay rise	fall
MUXOUT_1	output	1	5.12	4.18	0.72	0.77
MUXOUT_2	output	1	5.12	4.18	0.72	0.77
MUXOUT_3	output	1	5.12	4.18	0.72	0.77
MUXOUT_4	output	1	5.12	4.18	0.72	0.77
MUXOUT_5	output	1	5.12	4.18	0.72	0.77
MUXOUT_6	output	1	5.12	4.18	0.72	0.77
MUXOUT_7	output	1	5.12	4.18	0.72	0.77
MUXOUT_8	output	1	5.12	4.18	0.72	0.77
MUXOUT_9	output	1	5.12	4.18	0.72	0.77
MUXOUT_10	output	1	5.12	4.18	0.72	0.77
MUXOUT_11	output	1	5.12	4.18	0.72	0.77
MUXOUT_12	output	1	5.12	4.18	0.72	0.77

Number of ports: 63
Number of nets: 131
Number of cells: 80
Number of references: 6

Combinational area: 104.00
Noncombinational area: 0.00
Net Interconnect area: 0.00 (No wire load specified)

Total area: 104.00

Note that the critical path has been reduced to 5.12 nS (from 5.68), by increasing the gate count to 104 (from 69). By adjusting the design constraints to a compromise between the fastest and the smallest design, a speed/area trade-off design can be synthesized. The results of this optimization are shown below:

Operating Conditions:
Wire Loading Model:

Information: Updating design information. (UID-85)

Library(s) Used:
    CMOS_1.5 (File: /osi7/release/v1.2-beta2/libraries/
CMOS_1.5.db)

Number of ports: 63
Number of nets: 107
Number of cells: 56
Number of references: 6

Combinational area: 81.00
Noncombinational area: 0.00
Net Interconnect area: 0.00   (No wire load specified)
Total area: 81.00

****

Report : timing
     -path end
     -delay max
Design : Y
Version: 1.2-beta2
Date   : Mon Sep 4 20:15:32 1989
****

Operating Conditions:
Wire Loading Model:

Point	Type	Fanout	Max Delay		Min Delay	
			rise	fall	rise	fall
MUXOUT_1	output	1	5.34	3.51	0.74	0.70
MUXOUT_2	output	1	5.34	3.51	0.74	0.70
MUXOUT_3	output	1	5.34	3.51	0.74	0.70
MUXOUT_4	output	1	5.34	3.51	0.74	0.70
MUXOUT_5	output	1	5.34	3.51	0.74	0.70
MUXOUT_6	output	1	5.34	3.51	0.74	0.70
MUXOUT_7	output	1	5.34	3.51	0.74	0.70
MUXOUT_8	output	1	5.34	3.51	0.74	0.70
MUXOUT_9	output	1	5.34	3.51	0.74	0.70
MUXOUT_10	output	1	5.34	3.51	0.74	0.70
MUXOUT_11	output	1	5.34	3.51	0.74	0.70
MUXOUT_12	output	1	5.34	3.51	0.74	0.70

Here we see that the tool was able to find a design that had a critical path length of 5.34 nS while using just 81 gates.

Following are the results of the three optimization runs summarized graphically. The schematics of each design have also been included at the end of this section.

Speed/Area Tradeoff for Module Y

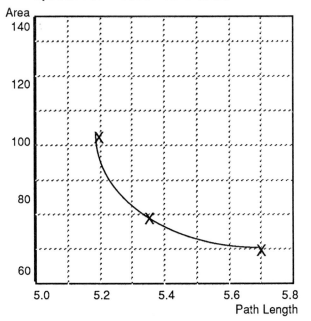

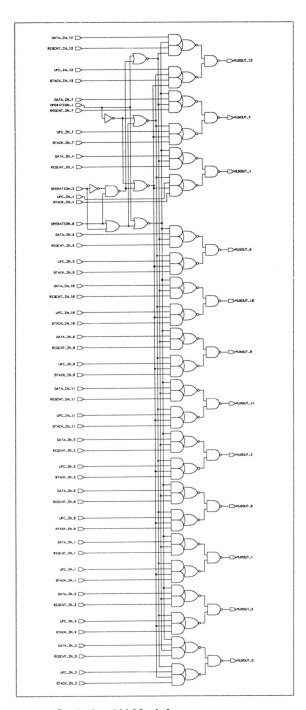

Area Optimized Y Module

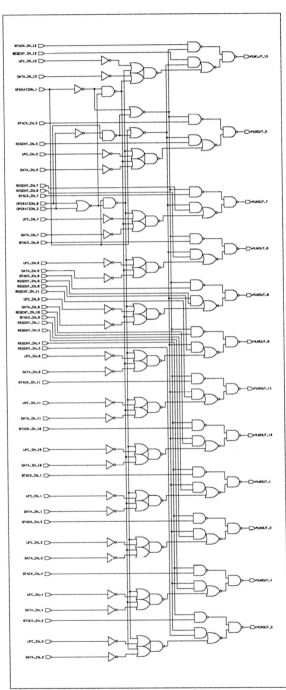

Speed Optimized Y Module

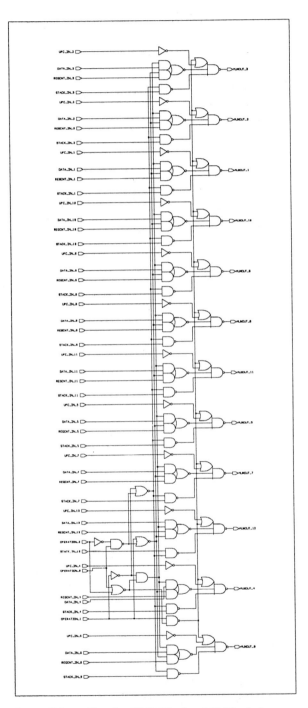

Speed/Area Tradeoff Optimized Y Module

Synthesis of the UPC Module

The UPC module consists of combinational logic as well as sequential elements. The original design was mapped using a 1.5 micron CMOS library. The original (mapped without constraints) UPC had a total area of 187 gate equivalents (84 sequential, 103 combinational) and a critical path delay of 16.28nSec. The UPC module was then optimized for area, and the following results were obtained:

Information: Updating design information. (UID-85)

****

Report : area
Design : UPC
Version: 1.2-beta2
Date   : Mon Sep 4 18:08:42 1989
****

Library(s) Used:

   CMOS_1.5 (File: /osi7/release/v1.2-beta2/libraries
     /CMOS_1.5.db)

Number of ports:	39
Number of nets:	80
Number of cells:	53
Number of references:	6

Combinational area:	66.00
Noncombinational area:	84.00
Net Interconnect area:	0.00 (No wire load specified)

Total area: 150.00

****

Report : timing
   -path end
   -delay max
Design : UPC
Version: 1.2-beta2
Date   : Mon Sep 4 18:08:42 1989
****

Operating Conditions:
Wire Loading Model:

Point	Type	Fanout	Max Delay rise	fall	Min Delay rise	fall
u3_1/D	FD1	1	11.15	10.46	1.77	1.24
u3_2/D	FD1	1	10.08	9.40	1.77	1.41
u3_3/D	FD1	1	9.70	9.01	1.77	1.24
u3_4/D	FD1	1	8.37	7.68	1.77	1.41
u3_5/D	FD1	1	7.99	7.30	1.77	1.24
u3_6/D	FD1	1	7.07	6.38	1.77	1.24
u3_7/D	FD1	1	5.75	5.06	1.77	1.41
u3_8/D	FD1	1	5.36	4.67	1.77	1.24
u3_9/D	FD1	1	4.19	3.50	1.77	1.41
u3_10/D	FD1	1	3.65	2.96	1.77	1.24
u3_11/D	FD1	1	2.85	2.16	1.77	1.41
u3_12/D	FD1	1	1.93	1.41	1.77	1.24

Point	Type	Fanout	Max Delay		Min Delay	
			rise	fall	rise	fall
OUTPUT_BAR_1	output	1	1.59	1.37	1.59	1.37
OUTPUT_BAR_2	output	1	1.59	1.37	1.59	1.37
OUTPUT_BAR_3	output	1	1.59	1.37	1.59	1.37
OUTPUT_BAR_4	output	1	1.59	1.37	1.59	1.37
OUTPUT_BAR_5	output	1	1.59	1.37	1.59	1.37
OUTPUT_BAR_6	output	1	1.59	1.37	1.59	1.37
OUTPUT_BAR_7	output	1	1.59	1.37	1.59	1.37
OUTPUT_BAR_8	output	1	1.59	1.37	1.59	1.37
OUTPUT_BAR_9	output	1	1.59	1.37	1.59	1.37
OUTPUT_BAR_10	output	1	1.59	1.37	1.59	1.37
OUTPUT_BAR_11	output	1	1.59	1.37	1.59	1.37
OUTPUT_BAR_12	output	1	1.59	1.37	1.59	1.37
OUTPUT_1	output	1	1.09	1.37	1.09	1.37
OUTPUT_2	output	1	1.09	1.37	1.09	1.37
OUTPUT_3	output	1	1.09	1.37	1.09	1.37
OUTPUT_4	output	1	1.09	1.37	1.09	1.37
OUTPUT_5	output	1	1.09	1.37	1.09	1.37
OUTPUT_6	output	1	1.09	1.37	1.09	1.37
OUTPUT_7	output	1	1.09	1.37	1.09	1.37
OUTPUT_8	output	1	1.09	1.37	1.09	1.37
OUTPUT_9	output	1	1.09	1.37	1.09	1.37
OUTPUT_10	output	1	1.09	1.37	1.09	1.37
OUTPUT_11	output	1	1.09	1.37	1.09	1.37
OUTPUT_12	output	1	1.09	1.37	1.09	1.37

As shown in the area optimized results, the critical path delay has been reduced to 11.15 nS with a gate count of 150.

The UPC module was then optimized for speed, and the following results were obtained:

Information: Updating design information. (UID-85)

```
****************************************
Report : area
Design : UPC
Version: 1.2-beta3
Date   : Fri Sep 15 07:53:33 1989
****************************************
```

Library(s) Used:

   CMOS_1.5 (File: /osi2/src/dc/libraries/CMOS_1.5.db)

Number of ports:	39
Number of nets:	242
Number of cells:	215
Number of references:	17

Combinational area:	336.00	
Noncombinational area:	84.00	
Net Interconnect area:	0.00	(No wire load specified)

Total area:	420.00

```
****************************************
Report : timing
       -path end
       -delay max
Design : UPC
Version: 1.2-beta3
Date   : Fri Sep 15 07:53:33 1989
****************************************
```

Operating Conditions:
Wire Loading Model:

Point	Type	Fanout	Max Delay rise	Max Delay fall	Min Delay rise	Min Delay fall
u3_1/D	FD1	1	3.12	3.28	1.34	1.85
u3_2/D	FD1	1	3.12	3.28	1.34	1.85
u3_3/D	FD1	1	3.19	3.15	1.34	1.85
u3_6/D	FD1	1	2.71	3.05	1.01	1.23
u3_5/D	FD1	1	2.75	3.05	1.34	1.38
u3_4/D	FD1	1	2.68	3.05	1.34	1.38
u3_7/D	FD1	1	2.90	2.77	1.01	1.23
u3_8/D	FD1	1	2.90	2.77	1.01	1.23
u3_9/D	FD1	1	2.70	2.58	1.01	1.23
u3_10/D	FD1	1	2.57	2.22	1.01	1.23
u3_11/D	FD1	1	2.29	1.98	0.96	1.07
u3_12/D	FD1	1	2.03	1.55	0.85	0.85

Point	Type	Fanout	Max Delay rise	Max Delay fall	Min Delay rise	Min Delay fall
OUTPUT_BAR_1	output	1	1.59	1.37	1.59	1.37
OUTPUT_BAR_2	output	1	1.59	1.37	1.59	1.37
OUTPUT_BAR_3	output	1	1.59	1.37	1.59	1.37
OUTPUT_BAR_4	output	1	1.59	1.37	1.59	1.37
OUTPUT_BAR_5	output	1	1.59	1.37	1.59	1.37
OUTPUT_BAR_6	output	1	1.59	1.37	1.59	1.37
OUTPUT_BAR_7	output	1	1.59	1.37	1.59	1.37
OUTPUT_BAR_8	output	1	1.59	1.37	1.59	1.37
OUTPUT_BAR_9	output	1	1.59	1.37	1.59	1.37
OUTPUT_BAR_10	output	1	1.59	1.37	1.59	1.37
OUTPUT_BAR_11	output	1	1.59	1.37	1.59	1.37
OUTPUT_BAR_12	output	1	1.59	1.37	1.59	1.37
OUTPUT_1	output	1	1.09	1.37	1.09	1.37
OUTPUT_2	output	1	1.09	1.37	1.09	1.37
OUTPUT_3	output	1	1.09	1.37	1.09	1.37
OUTPUT_4	output	1	1.09	1.37	1.09	1.37
OUTPUT_5	output	1	1.09	1.37	1.09	1.37
OUTPUT_6	output	1	1.09	1.37	1.09	1.37
OUTPUT_7	output	1	1.09	1.37	1.09	1.37
OUTPUT_8	output	1	1.09	1.37	1.09	1.37
OUTPUT_9	output	1	1.09	1.37	1.09	1.37
OUTPUT_10	output	1	1.09	1.37	1.09	1.37
OUTPUT_11	output	1	1.09	1.37	1.09	1.37
OUTPUT_12	output	1	1.09	1.37	1.09	1.37

The speed optimized version of the UPC module has a critical path delay of 3.28 nS, the area, however, has been increased to 420 gates. The area optimized and speed optimized versions make up the endpoints of the design curve.

The midpoint of the design curve is obtained by specifying a clock period greater than zero nS and less than 100 nS. The results of the midpoint optimization are as follows:

Information: Updating design information. (UID-85)

```
******************************************
Report : area
Design : UPC
Version: 1.2-beta2
Date   : Mon Sep  4 19:38:33 1989
******************************************
```

Library(s) Used:

    CMOS_1.5 (File: /osi7/release/v1.2-beta2/libraries
       /CMOS_1.5.db)

Number of ports:	39
Number of nets:	80
Number of cells:	53
Number of references:	9
Combinational area:	79.00
Noncombinational area:	96.00
Net Interconnect area:	0.00 (No wire load specified)
Total area:	175.00

```
******************************************
Report : timing
    -path end
    -delay max
Design : UPC
Version: 1.2-beta2
Date   : Mon Sep  4 19:38:33 1989
******************************************
```

Operating Conditions:
Wire Loading Model:

Point	Type	Fanout	Max Delay		Min Delay	
			rise	fall	rise	fall
u3_1/D	FD1P	1	8.90	9.27	0.62	0.82
u3_2/D	FD1P	1	8.32	8.71	0.62	0.82
u3_3/D	FD1P	1	7.91	8.30	0.62	0.82
u3_4/D	FD1P	1	7.14	7.53	0.62	0.82
u3_5/D	FD1P	1	6.77	7.16	0.62	0.82
u3_6/D	FD1P	1	6.00	6.38	0.62	0.82
u3_7/D	FD1P	1	4.94	5.33	0.62	0.82
u3_8/D	FD1P	1	4.55	4.94	0.62	0.82
u3_9/D	FD1P	1	3.78	4.17	0.62	0.82
u3_10/D	FD1P	1	3.41	3.80	0.62	0.82
u3_11/D	FD1P	1	2.63	3.02	0.62	0.82
u3_12/D	FD1P	1	1.54	1.91	0.62	0.82
					(Continued Over)	

Point	Type	Fanout	Max rise	Delay fall	Min rise	Delay fall
OUTPUT_BAR_1	output	1	1.84	1.74	1.84	1.74
OUTPUT_BAR_2	output	1	1.84	1.74	1.84	1.74
OUTPUT_BAR_3	output	1	1.84	1.74	1.84	1.74
OUTPUT_BAR_4	output	1	1.84	1.74	1.84	1.74
OUTPUT_BAR_5	output	1	1.84	1.74	1.84	1.74
OUTPUT_BAR_6	output	1	1.84	1.74	1.84	1.74
OUTPUT_BAR_7	output	1	1.84	1.74	1.84	1.74
OUTPUT_BAR_8	output	1	1.84	1.74	1.84	1.74
OUTPUT_BAR_9	output	1	1.84	1.74	1.84	1.74
OUTPUT_BAR_10	output	1	1.84	1.74	1.84	1.74
OUTPUT_BAR_11	output	1	1.84	1.74	1.84	1.74
OUTPUT_BAR_12	output	1	1.84	1.74	1.84	1.74
OUTPUT_1	output	1	1.16	1.44	1.16	1.44
OUTPUT_2	output	1	1.16	1.44	1.16	1.44
OUTPUT_3	output	1	1.16	1.44	1.16	1.44
OUTPUT_4	output	1	1.16	1.44	1.16	1.44
OUTPUT_5	output	1	1.16	1.44	1.16	1.44
OUTPUT_6	output	1	1.16	1.44	1.16	1.44
OUTPUT_7	output	1	1.16	1.44	1.16	1.44
OUTPUT_8	output	1	1.16	1.44	1.16	1.44
OUTPUT_9	output	1	1.16	1.44	1.16	1.44
OUTPUT_10	output	1	1.16	1.44	1.16	1.44
OUTPUT_11	output	1	1.16	1.44	1.16	1.44
OUTPUT_12	output	1	1.16	1.44	1.16	1.44

The trade-off optimization yields a design with 175 gates and a critical path length of 9.27 nS. The results of the three optimizations, and the generated schematics are given below.

Speed/Area Tradeoff for Module UPC

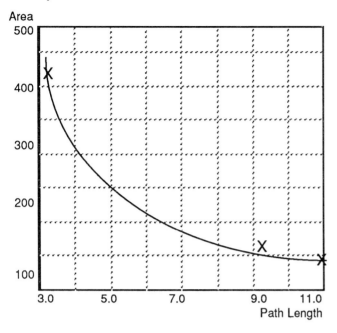

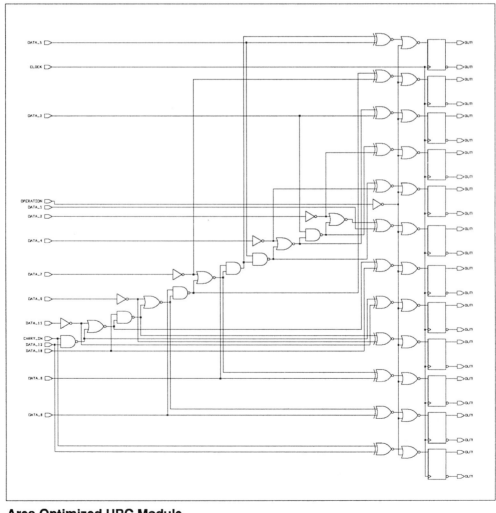

Area Optimized UPC Module

Speed/Area Optimized UPC Module

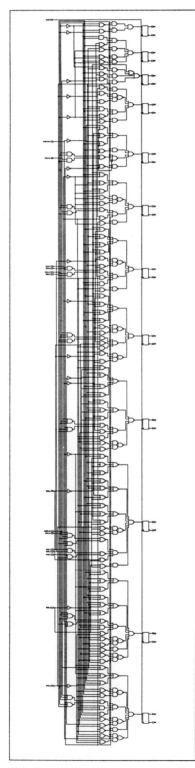

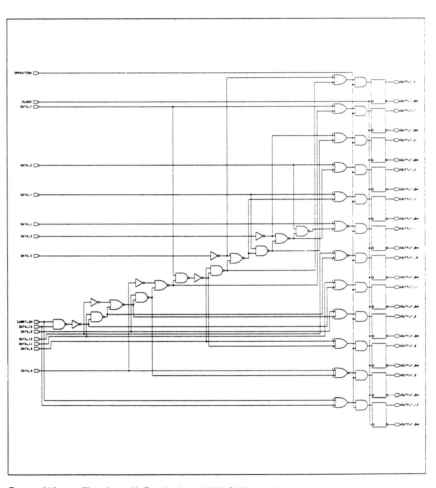

Speed/Area Trade-off Optimized UPC Module

Synthesis of the RegCnt Module

The REGCNT module contains both an increment and a load operation. This sequential part requires both a clock speed design goal, and an output signal arrival time goal. The same procedure is followed to obtain three designs for this module.

The first optimization is the area-only run, whose results are shown below.

Information: Updating design information. (UID-85)

```
*****************************************
Report : area
Design : REGCNT
Version: 1.2-beta2
Date   : Mon Sep  4 18:09:03 1989
*****************************************
```

Library(s) Used:

    CMOS_1.5 (File: /osi7/release/v1.2-beta2/libraries
        /CMOS_1.5.db)

Number of ports:	28
Number of nets:	103
Number of cells:	77
Number of references:	14

Combinational area: 102.00
Noncombinational area: 84.00
Net Interconnect area: 0.00 (No wire load specified)

Total area: 186.00

```
*****************************************
Report : timing
   -path end
   -delay max
Design : REGCNT
Version: 1.2-beta2
Date   : Mon Sep  4 18:09:03 1989
*****************************************
```

Operating Conditions:
Wire Loading Model:

Point	Type	Fanout	Max Delay rise	fall	Min Delay rise	fall
u3_1/D	FD1	1	11.58	12.73	1.09	0.82
u3_2/D	FD1	1	11.34	12.59	1.09	0.82
u3_3/D	FD1	1	10.99	11.94	1.00	1.14
u3_4/D	FD1	1	9.86	10.71	1.00	1.14
u3_5/D	FD1	1	8.61	9.54	1.00	1.14
u3_6/D	FD1	1	8.39	8.83	1.00	1.14
u3_7/D	FD1	1	7.37	7.48	1.00	1.14
u3_8/D	FD1	1	6.52	6.42	1.09	0.82
ZERO	output	2	6.12	4.23	3.11	1.84
u3_9/D	FD1	1	5.77	5.77	1.00	1.14
u3_11/D	FD1	1	4.78	3.90	1.09	0.82
u3_10/D	FD1	1	4.78	4.55	1.00	1.14
u3_12/D	FD1	1	4.50	2.80	1.09	0.82

Continued Over

Point	Type	Fanout	Max Delay rise	fall	Min Delay rise	fall
OUTPUT_4	output	4	1.53	1.53	1.53	1.53
OUTPUT_7	output	4	1.53	1.53	1.53	1.53
OUTPUT_8	output	4	1.53	1.53	1.53	1.53
OUTPUT_10	output	4	1.53	1.53	1.53	1.53
OUTPUT_12	output	4	1.53	1.53	1.53	1.53
OUTPUT_2	output	3	1.38	1.47	1.38	1.47
OUTPUT_5	output	3	1.38	1.47	1.38	1.47
OUTPUT_6	output	3	1.38	1.47	1.38	1.47
OUTPUT_1	output	2	1.24	1.42	1.24	1.42
OUTPUT_3	output	2	1.24	1.42	1.24	1.42
OUTPUT_11	output	2	1.24	1.42	1.24	1.42
OUTPUT_9	output	1	1.09	1.37	1.09	1.37

The critical path delay for the area optimized network is 12.73 nS, with a gate count of 186.

Next the Design Compiler was asked to create the fastest design possible without regard to the resulting area. The timing/ area report for this run is shown below:

Information: Updating design information. (UID-85)
****

Report : area
Design : REGCNT
Version: 1.2-beta2
Date   : Mon Sep 4 18:41:38 1989
****

Library(s) Used:
    CMOS_1.5 (File: /osi7/release/v1.2-beta2/libraries/
CMOS_1.5.db)

Number of ports: 28
Number of nets: 142
Number of cells: 115
Number of references: 24

Combinational area: 163.00
Noncombinational area: 92.00
Net Interconnect area: 0.00
(No wire load specified)

Total area: 255.00

****
Report : timing
    -path end
    -delay max
Design : REGCNT
Version: 1.2-beta2
Date   : Mon Sep 4 18:41:38 1989
****

Operating Conditions:
Wire Loading Model:

Point	Type	Fanout	Max Delay rise	fall	Min Delay rise	fall
u3_4/D	FD1P	1	7.09	7.69	1.77	1.63
u3_1/D	FD1P	1	6.63	7.62	1.19	1.30
u3_2/D	FD1	1	7.01	7.61	1.69	1.30
u3_5/D	FD1P	1	7.01	7.36	1.69	1.30
u3_3/D	FD1P	1	7.01	7.20	1.69	1.30
u3_6/D	FD1P	1	7.11	7.10	1.33	1.53
u3_8/D	FD1P	1	6.91	7.10	1.13	1.53
u3_7/D	FD1	1	6.97	6.86	1.19	1.30
u3_10/D	FD1P	1	5.88	6.04	1.35	1.71
u3_9/D	FD1	1	5.72	5.68	1.19	1.30
u3_11/D	FD1	1	4.93	4.47	1.00	1.14

Point	Type	Fanout	Max Delay rise	Max Delay fall	Min Delay rise	Min Delay fall
ZERO	output	2	4.06	4.04	3.49	3.56
u3_12/D	FD1P	1	3.87	3.58	1.09	0.82
OUTPUT_7	output	2	1.95	2.22	1.95	2.22
OUTPUT_1	output	3	1.42	1.58	1.42	1.58
OUTPUT_6	output	5	1.42	1.58	1.42	1.58
OUTPUT_10	output	4	1.42	1.58	1.42	1.58
OUTPUT_12	output	4	1.42	1.58	1.42	1.58
OUTPUT_3	output	4	1.36	1.54	1.36	1.54
OUTPUT_4	output	3	1.36	1.54	1.36	1.54
OUTPUT_5	output	3	1.36	1.54	1.36	1.54
OUTPUT_8	output	3	1.36	1.54	1.36	1.54
OUTPUT_2	output	3	1.38	1.47	1.38	1.47
OUTPUT_9	output	2	1.24	1.42	1.24	1.42
OUTPUT_11	output	2	1.24	1.42	1.24	1.42

Number of ports: 28
Number of nets: 119
Number of cells: 92
Number of references: 20

Combinational area: 118.00
Noncombinational area: 84.00
Net Interconnect area: 0.00
(No wire load specified)
Total area: 202.00

****

Report : timing
   -path end
   -delay max
Design : REGCNT
Version: 1.2-beta2
Date   : Mon Sep 4 19:50:37 1989
****

Operating Conditions:
Wire Loading Model:

The speed optimized network has a critical path length of 7.69 nS while using 255 gates to achieve this speed.

The final optimization on REGCNT is performed to obtain the design space trade-off point. The results of this optimization are shown below:

Information: Updating design information. (UID-85)
****

Report : area
Design : REGCNT
Version: 1.2-beta2
Date   : Mon Sep 4 19:50:37 1989
****

Library(s) Used:
   CMOS_1.5 (File: /osi7/release/v1.2-beta2/libraries
     /CMOS_1.5.db)

Point	Type	Fanout	Max Delay rise	Max Delay fall	Min Delay rise	Min Delay fall
u3_1/D	FD1	1	9.78	9.86	0.99	1.30
u3_2/D	FD1	1	9.55	9.72	1.19	1.30
u3_3/D	FD1	1	9.46	9.31	1.19	1.30
u3_4/D	FD1	1	7.62	8.38	1.33	1.53
u3_5/D	FD1	1	7.33	7.71	1.19	1.30
u3_6/D	FD1	1	6.41	6.78	1.84	1.53
u3_7/D	FD1	1	6.36	6.11	1.19	1.30
u3_8/D	FD1	1	5.35	5.46	1.00	1.14
u3_10/D	FD1	1	5.13	4.47	1.33	1.53
u3_9/D	FD1	1	4.99	4.74	1.19	1.30
u3_11/D	FD1	1	4.12	3.81	1.00	1.14

Point	Type	Fanout	Max Delay rise	Max Delay fall	Min Delay rise	Min Delay fall
ZERO	output	1	3.96	3.80	3.07	2.49
u3_12/D	FD1	1	3.69	2.92	1.09	0.82
OUTPUT_7	output	2	2.00	2.09	2.00	2.09
OUTPUT_9	output	4	1.67	1.58	1.67	1.58
OUTPUT_12	output	5	1.67	1.58	1.67	1.58
OUTPUT_10	output	3	1.53	1.53	1.53	1.53
OUTPUT_1	output	3	1.38	1.47	1.38	1.47
OUTPUT_2	output	3	1.38	1.47	1.38	1.47
OUTPUT_4	output	3	1.38	1.47	1.38	1.47
OUTPUT_5	output	3	1.38	1.47	1.38	1.47
OUTPUT_6	output	2	1.38	1.47	1.38	1.47
OUTPUT_11	output	3	1.38	1.47	1.38	1.47
OUTPUT_8	output	2	1.24	1.42	1.24	1.42
OUTPUT_3	output	1	1.09	1.37	1.09	1.37

The design space midpoint computed during optimization used 202 gates to achieve a critical path length of 9.86 nS.

Following are the results of three optimization runs summarized graphically with the corresponding schematics.

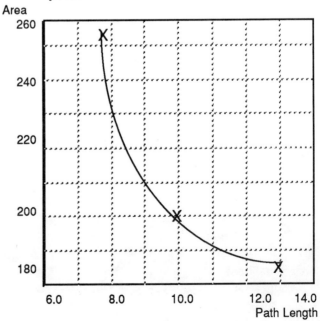

Speed/Area Tradeoff for Module REGCNT

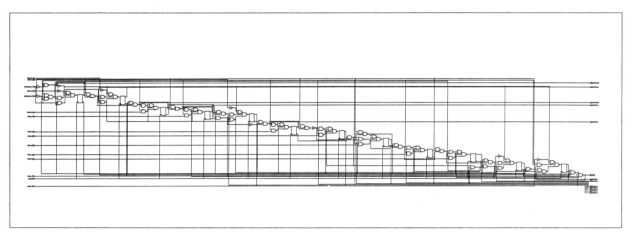

Area Optimized REGCNT Module

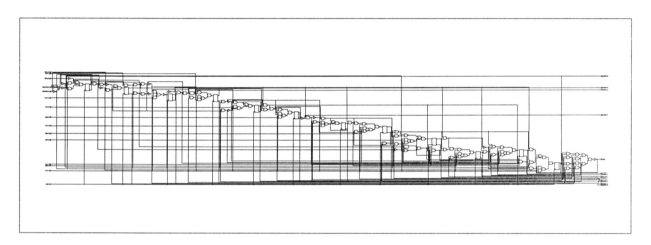

Speed Optimized REGCNT

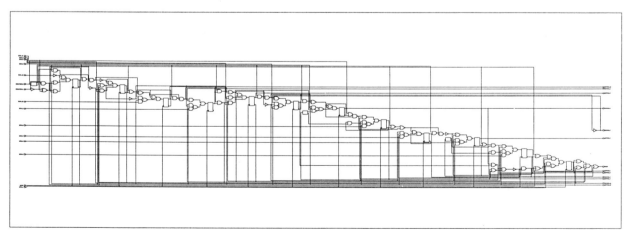

Speed/Area Tradeoff Optimized REGCNT Module

Synthesis of the Control Module

The CONTROL module is unique in that the smallest design is also the fastest design. This means that for the target technology library there is no speed area trade-off to be made. There are not many designs descriptions that yield this kind of a solution. Following are the results of the optimization run.

```
*****************************************
Report : timing
   -path end
   -delay max
Design : CONTROL
Version: 1.2-beta2
Date   : Mon Sep  4 18:09:21 1989
*****************************************
```

Operating Conditions:
Wire Loading Model:

Information: Updating design information. (UID-85)

```
*****************************************
Report : area
Design : CONTROL
Version: 1.2-beta2
Date   : Mon Sep  4 18:09:21 1989
*****************************************
```

Library(s) Used:

  CMOS_1.5 (File: /osi7/release /v1.2-beta2/libraries/CMOS_1.5.db)

Number of ports:	19
Number of nets:	54
Number of cells:	46
Number of references:	12

Combinational area:	64.00
Noncombinational area:	0.00
Net Interconnect area:	0.00
(No wire load specified)	

Total area:	64.00

Point	Type	Fanout	Max Delay rise	fall	Min Delay rise	fall
STACK_CONTROL_1	output	1	4.10	4.04	1.27	1.18
Y_CONTROL_0	output	1	3.90	3.07	1.88	1.20
Y_CONTROL_1	output	1	3.60	3.60	0.74	1.03
REGCNT_CONTROL_0	output	1	3.01	3.59	0.92	0.37
STACK_CONTROL_0	output	1	3.45	2.93	1.55	1.30
REGCNT_CONTROL_1	output	1	2.68	1.85	1.11	0.27
UPC_CONTROL	output	1	2.21	2.39	1.92	2.03
MAPPING_ROM_ENABLE	output	1	2.19	1.93	1.04	0.73
INTERRUPT_VECTOR_ENABLE	output	1	2.19	1.93	0.50	0.13
Y_CONTROL_2	output	2	2.14	1.97	1.78	1.68
PIPELINE_ENABLE	output	3	1.80	1.69	0.98	0.97

The optimized design uses just 64 gates and has a critical path length of 4.10 nS. The synthesis tool was unable to beat itself in terms of speed or area using the outlined procedure. Following is a schematic for this design.

Speed/Area Optimized CONTROL Module

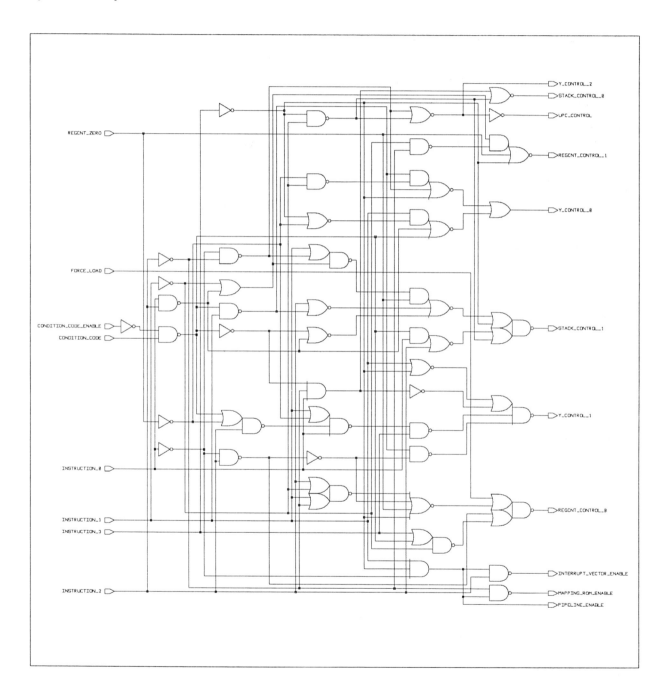

Synthesis of the Stack Module

The STACK module is the largest module in the 2910 in terms of resulting gate count. This is the module that has the 9-deep by 12-bit word storage elements built out of flip/flop, three-buffer pairs. The surrounding control logic is the only circuitry that can be optimized for speed-area trade-offs. The SUB_ELEMENT hierarchy has been maintained during each optimization.

The results of the area-only optimization are given first.

Information: Updating design information. (UID-85)
****

Report : area
Design : STACK
Version: 1.2-beta2
Date   : Tue Sep 5 17:34:31 1989
****

Library(s) Used:

CMOS_1.5 (File: /osi7/release/v1.2-beta2
/libraries/CMOS_1.5.db)

Number of ports:	28
Number of nets:	142
Number of cells:	116
Number of references:	19

Combinational area:	489.00
Noncombinational area:	812.00
Net Interconnect area:	0.00
(No wire load specified)	
Total area:	1301.00

****

Report : timing
    -path end
    -delay max
Design : STACK
Version: 1.2-beta2
Date   : Tue Sep 5 17:34:31 1989
****

Operating Conditions:
Wire Loading Model:

Point	Type	Fanout	Max Delay		Min Delay	
			rise	fall	rise	fall
OUTPUT_VALUE_1	output	1	11.74	11.50	4.16	3.93
OUTPUT_VALUE_2	output	1	11.74	11.50	4.16	3.93
OUTPUT_VALUE_3	output	1	11.74	11.50	4.16	3.93
OUTPUT_VALUE_4	output	1	11.74	11.50	4.16	3.93
OUTPUT_VALUE_5	output	1	11.74	11.50	4.16	3.93
OUTPUT_VALUE_6	output	1	11.74	11.50	4.16	3.93
OUTPUT_VALUE_7	output	1	11.74	11.50	4.16	3.93
OUTPUT_VALUE_8	output	1	11.74	11.50	4.16	3.93
OUTPUT_VALUE_9	output	1	11.74	11.50	4.16	3.93
OUTPUT_VALUE_10	output	1	11.74	11.50	4.16	3.93
OUTPUT_VALUE_11	output	1	11.74	11.50	4.16	3.93
OUTPUT_VALUE_12	output	1	11.74	11.50	4.16	3.93
u179_2/D	FD1	1	10.16	6.18	1.17	1.13
u180_2/D	FD1	1	7.44	10.10	1.94	1.94
u180_1/D	FD1	1	8.90	8.54	1.52	1.63
u180_3/D	FD1	1	6.65	8.55	1.51	2.31
u180_0/D	FD1	1	7.10	6.36	1.17	1.29
u179_1/D	FD1	1	6.79	5.26	1.18	0.45
u179_3/D	FD1	1	5.97	5.97	2.64	0.92
u179_0/D	FD1	1	5.53	5.19	0.78	0.50
OVERFLOW	output	1	4.09	4.64	2.96	2.28
U5/u28_7/D	FD1	0	0.00	0.00	0.00	0.00
U5/u28_10/D	FD1	0	0.00	0.00	0.00	0.00
U5/u28_11/D	FD1	0	0.00	0.00	0.00	0.00
(Listing Truncated)						

The area optimization yields a design of 1301 gates and a critical path length (from flip/flop to module output) of 11.74 nS. The next optimization run was seeking to find the smallest possible design. The timing/area report is shown on the next page.

Information: Updating design information.
(UID-85)

```
*****************************************

Report : area
Design : STACK
Version: 1.2-beta2
Date   : Tue Sep  5 18:06:28 1989
*****************************************

Library(s) Used:

    CMOS_1.5 (File: /osi7/release/v1.2-beta2
/libraries/CMOS_1.5.db)


Number of ports:        28
Number of nets:         178
Number of cells:        148
Number of references:   31


Combinational area:     540.00
Noncombinational area:  818.00
Net Interconnect area:  0.00 (No wire load specified)


Total area:             1358.00


*****************************************

Report : timing
     -path end
     -delay max
Design : STACK
Version: 1.2-beta2
Date   : Tue Sep  5 18:06:28 1989
*****************************************

Operating Conditions:
Wire Loading Model:

                    Max Delay
```

Min Delay Point	Type	Fanout	rise	fall	rise	fall
OUTPUT_VALUE_1	output	1	9.00	8.57	4.32	4.08
OUTPUT_VALUE_2	output	1	9.00	8.57	4.32	4.08
OUTPUT_VALUE_3	output	1	9.00	8.57	4.32	4.08
OUTPUT_VALUE_4	output	1	9.00	8.57	4.32	4.08
OUTPUT_VALUE_5	output	1	9.00	8.57	4.32	4.08
OUTPUT_VALUE_6	output	1	9.00	8.57	4.32	4.08
OUTPUT_VALUE_7	output	1	9.00	8.57	4.32	4.08
OUTPUT_VALUE_8	output	1	9.00	8.57	4.32	4.08
OUTPUT_VALUE_9	output	1	9.00	8.57	4.32	4.08
OUTPUT_VALUE_10	output	1	9.00	8.57	4.32	4.08
OUTPUT_VALUE_11	output	1	9.00	8.57	4.32	4.08
OUTPUT_VALUE_12	output	1	9.00	8.57	4.32	4.08
u180_2/D	FD1P	1	6.12	6.06	2.11	2.40
u180_1/D	FD1	1	6.01	6.11	0.78	0.50
u180_3/D	FD1P	1	5.73	6.02	1.88	1.87
u180_0/D	FD1	1	5.81	5.98	1.21	1.43
u179_1/D	FD1P	1	5.06	4.87	1.74	1.63
u179_2/D	FD1P	1	4.74	4.73	1.21	1.49
OVERFLOW	output	1	4.21	4.44	2.37	2.38
u179_3/D	FD1P	1	4.16	4.43	2.03	1.78
u179_0/D	FD1P	1	4.04	4.30	1.23	1.03
U6/u28_6/D	FD1	0	0.00	0.00	0.00	0.00
U6/u28_5/D	FD1	0	0.00	0.00	0.00	0.00
U6/u28_4/D	FD1	0	0.00	0.00	0.00	0.00
U6/u28_12/D	FD1	0	0.00	0.00	0.00	0.00
U6/u28_7/D	FD1	0	0.00	0.00	0.00	0.00
U6/u28_10/D	FD1	0	0.00	0.00	0.00	0.00
(Listing Truncated)						

The speed only optimization yields a design of
1358 gates with a critical path of 9.00 nS.
The last STACK optimization was performed
to find a speed-area trade-off de-sign compromise. These results are listed below.

Information: Updating design information. (UID-85)

****

Report : area
Design : STACK
Version: 1.2-beta2
Date   : Tue Sep 5 19:01:44 1989
****

Library(s) Used:

   CMOS_1.5 (File: /osi7/release/v1.2-beta2
       /libraries/CMOS_1.5.db)

Number of ports: 28
Number of nets: 156
Number of cells: 130
Number of references: 25

Combinational area: 507.00
Noncombinational area: 812.00
Net Interconnect area: 0.00
(No wire load specified)
Total area: 1319.00

****

Report : timing
    -path end
    -delay max
Design : STACK
Version: 1.2-beta2
Date   : Tue Sep 5 19:01:44 1989
****

Operating Conditions:
Wire Loading Model:

Point	Type	Fanout	Max Delay rise	fall	Min Delay rise	fall
OUTPUT_VALUE_1	output	1	9.93	9.53	3.97	3.54
OUTPUT_VALUE_2	output	1	9.93	9.53	3.97	3.54
OUTPUT_VALUE_3	output	1	9.93	9.53	3.97	3.54
OUTPUT_VALUE_4	output	1	9.93	9.53	3.97	3.54
OUTPUT_VALUE_5	output	1	9.93	9.53	3.97	3.54
OUTPUT_VALUE_6	output	1	9.93	9.53	3.97	3.54
OUTPUT_VALUE_7	output	1	9.93	9.53	3.97	3.54
OUTPUT_VALUE_8	output	1	9.93	9.53	3.97	3.54
OUTPUT_VALUE_9	output	1	9.93	9.53	3.97	3.54
OUTPUT_VALUE_10	output	1	9.93	9.53	3.97	3.54
OUTPUT_VALUE_11	output	1	9.93	9.53	3.97	3.54
OUTPUT_VALUE_12	output	1	9.93	9.53	3.97	3.54
u180_2/D	FD1	1	7.15	7.28	2.41	1.94
u180_3/D	FD1	1	6.81	7.15	1.81	1.81
u180_1/D	FD1	1	7.00	6.87	0.78	0.50
u180_0/D	FD1	1	6.87	6.58	1.17	1.37
u179_1/D	FD1	1	6.45	6.09	1.72	2.24
u179_2/D	FD1	1	5.43	5.76	1.17	1.42
u179_3/D	FD1	1	4.76	5.46	1.96	1.72
OVERFLOW	output	1	5.04	5.43	3.13	2.46
u179_0/D	FD1	1	5.12	4.48	1.23	1.03
U6/u28_6/D	FD1	0	0.00	0.00	0.00	0.00
U6/u28_5/D	FD1	0	0.00	0.00	0.00	0.00
U6/u28_4/D	FD1	0	0.00	0.00	0.00	0.00
(Listing truncated)						

The trade-off found during optimization is a design with 1319 gates, and a critical path length of 9.93 nS.

The results of all three optimization runs are summarized on the next page with the corresponding network schematics.

Speed/Area Tradeoff for Module STACK

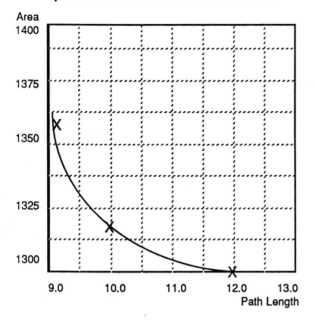

STACK Element Module

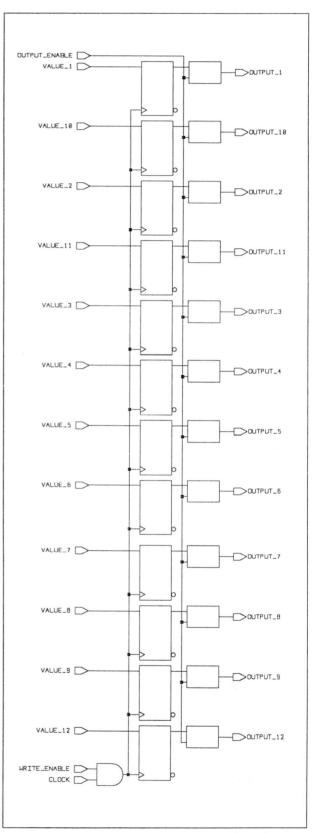

Area Optimized STACK Module

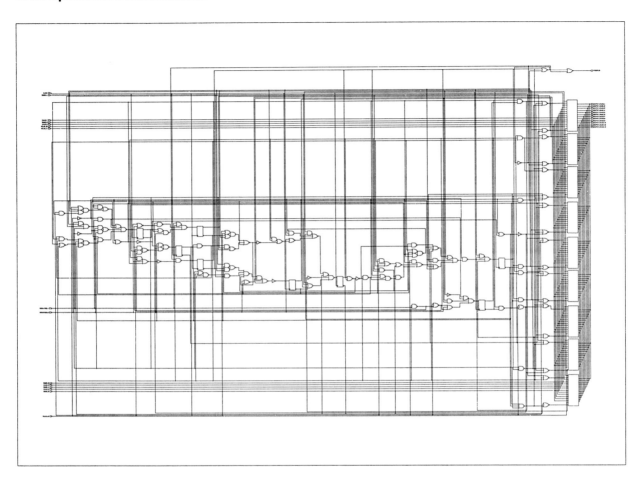

Speed Optimized STACK Module

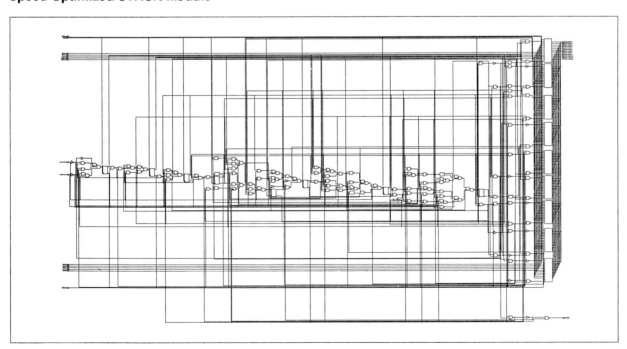

Speed/AreaTrade-off Optimized STACK Module

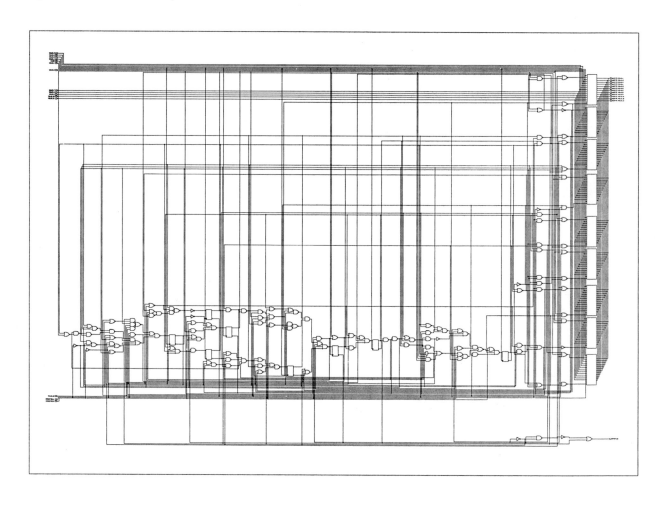

AM2910A Synthesis

At this point in the design cycle, all five of the 2910 modules have been translated into gates and optimized for both speed and area criteria. There are number of different scenarios that could be followed to arrive at the final design solution. Because this is an exercise in demonstrating the HDL design methodology, rather than an actual design project with specific design goals (i.e., there is no specific clock speed requirement or die size), this section will show how the lower level building blocks might be used to complete a design task.

The first approach to take is to use the existing modules to form three overall design solution points. By taking all of the area only results and combining them, we get the smallest 2910 that can be built with the pre-synthesized sub-modules. Similarly, we can create a design using just the speed-only optimized blocks, and the speed/area trade-off blocks. This approach allows the maintenance of the design hierarchy, because we are using the individually synthesized modules. The designs resulting from these compositions are summarized below.

Results maintaining hierarchy:

	Area	Delay_to_Output	Delay_to_F/F
smallest	1770	52.86	76.74
trade-off	1841	42.91	61.47
fastest	2201	43.88	50.36

The delay_to_output column is the delay from a primary input to an output port, and the delay_to_output column is the delay to a flip-flop data input pin. These delays are across the entire 2910.

Note that these numbers are for worst case commercial operating conditions, and with 10x10 die size used for wire length estimation.

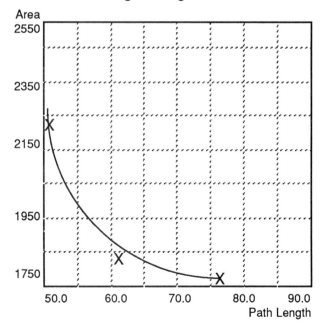

AM2910 Using Existing Blocks

151

The next optimization consists of an incremental-only mapping to the overall design. This optimization will remove the design hierarchy and find small incremental changes that can be made across module boundaries to improve the design quality. We try this operation to make an even 'smaller smallest' design, and an even faster fastest design.

Results using incremental only mapping:

	Area	Delay_to_Output	Delay_to_F/F
smallest	1768	52.86	76.74
trade-off	1809	36.35	55.00
fastest	2275	29.77	38.08

Note that these numbers are for worst case commercial operating conditions, and with 10x10 die size used for wire length estimation.

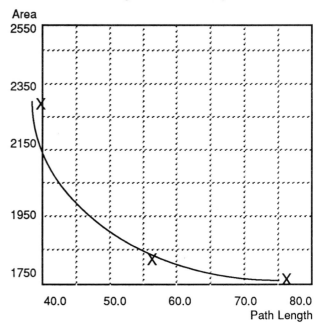

AM2910 Using Incremental Optimization

The next optimization consists of applying the optimizer on the whole design. This optimization will remove the design hierarchy to and treat the design as if it is one large random sequential boolean network. We try this operation to make an even 'smaller smallest' design, and an even 'faster fastest' design.

Results optimizing the entire design:

	Area	Delay_to_Output	Delay_to_F/F
smallest	2058	36.50	51.61
trade-off	2219	33.47	44.20
fastest	2892	29.58	34.69

Note that these numbers are for worst case commercial operating conditions, and with 10x10 die size used for wire length estimation.

AM2910 Optimization with NO Hierarchy

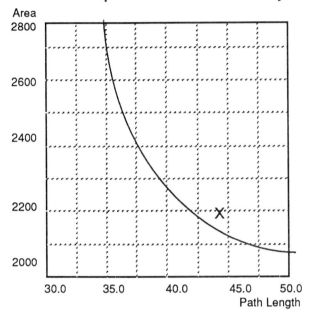

AM2910 Optimization Summary

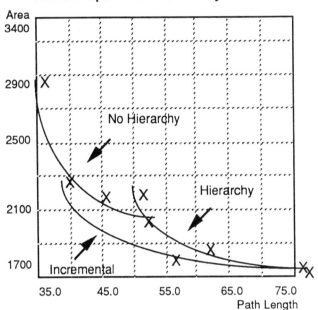

Another alternative in using the predefined modules is to mix and match the use of area and speed optimized modules. By using the timing report with the critical path delay option, the elements of critical paths can be reported. This shows which modules have system critical paths through them. We choose the fastest versions of these modules, and the smallest versions of the other modules to comprise the new design. There are other possibilities; the Design Compiler is setup to aid in the exploration of the design space.

The results of all three 2910 optimizations are summarized at right. The results show that the manipulation of the design hierarchy can play an important role in the exploration of the design trade-off space.

Am2910 Top-Level Design

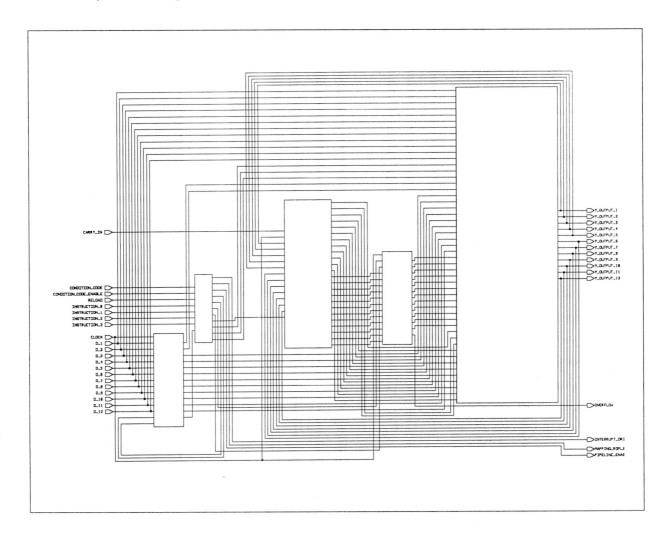

The Synopsys Standard Package: Synopsys.vhd

The VHDL option of the Synopsys HDL Compiler comes with a standard VHDL synthesis package. This package contains definitions for data types and op-erations on the data types that have widespread applica-bility in digital design. You are not requir-ed to use the types in this package. If you decide to use your own data types and operations, it is suggested that you follow the same conventions and style used in the standard synthesis package, SYNOPSYS.

This section does not contain the complete SYNOPSYS package, just those parts of the package that were needed for synthesizing the Am2910. In particular, for the 2910 design description the underlying data types used from this package were SIGNED, UNSIGNED, and INT (see the AMD project package section for more on how these are used). A function BIT_OF was used to convert a type BOOLEAN value into a BIT type. The operators "+" and "-" have been overloaded to perform addition and subtraction on the type UNSIGNED that was used for address arithmetic in the 2910 description. The complete standard package has been completed subsequent to the completion of this project, and has changed in its contents.

```vhdl
package SYNOPSYS is
  type UNSIGNED is array ( INTEGER range <>) of BIT;
  type SIGNED is array (INTEGER range <>) of BIT;
  subtype INT is INTEGER range -1 to 1;
  function BIT_OF (R : BOOLEAN) return BIT;
  function "+" ( L : UNSIGNED; R : INT) return UNSIGNED;
  function "+" ( L : UNSIGNED; R : BIT) return UNSIGNED;
  function "-" ( L : UNSIGNED; R : INT) return UNSIGNED;
end SYNOPSYS;

use WORK.SYNOPSYS.ALL;
package body SYNOPSYS is
```

```vhdl
function BIT_OF (R : BOOLEAN) return BIT is

begin
  case R is
    when TRUE  => return '1';
    when FALSE => return '0';
  end case;
end;
```

```vhdl
function "+" (L : UNSIGNED; R : INT)
return UNSIGNED is
  variable CARRY, VALUE : BIT;
  variable RESULT : UNSIGNED(L'LEFT to L'RIGHT);
begin
  case R is
    when -1 =>    VALUE := '1'; CARRY := '0';
    when 1 =>    VALUE := '0'; CARRY := '1';
    when others => VALUE := '0'; CARRY := '0';
  end case;
```

Overload function allows addition for bit vectors

```
for I in L'RIGHT downto L'LEFT loop
  RESULT(I) := L(I) xor VALUE xor CARRY;
  CARRY := (L(I) and VALUE) or (L(I) and CARRY) or
            (CARRY and VALUE);
end loop;
return RESULT;
end;
```

```
function "-" (L : UNSIGNED; R : INT) return UNSIGNED is
  begin
   return L + (-R);
  end;
```

```
function "+" (L : UNSIGNED; R : BIT) return UNSIGNED is
          variable TEMP : INT;
  begin
          if R = '0' then
            TEMP := 0;
        else
            TEMP := 1;
          end if;
          return L + TEMP;
  end;
end;
```

The 2910 Project Package:
Amd_pack.vhd

One of the fundamental aspects of team digital design is agreeing on interface conventions. VHDL packages are an excellent way to set down the conventions for a project in a concise unambiguous manner. The package is a global definition of data types, type conversions, and commonly used operations and functions, that become the design standard for a project.

For the 2910 design, a type ADDRESS is defined as the basic data type. An ADDRESS is the primary input and product of the 2910. It is a 12-bit bit vector. An array of addresses, ADDRESS_VECTOR is also defined to use for the test program ROM.

To simplify the initial interface specification, each module's control signals were coded as enumerated types of the possible operations for the module (INSTRUCTION_OPS, STACK_OPS, REGCNT_OPS, UPC_OPS, Y_MUX_OPS). Using an abstract type, decisions on control vector width and encoding could be deferred to the synthesis process. Also, the design description is inherently more understandable when dealing with symbolic operation names rather than operation codes.

A function WIRED_OR was defined as the bus resolution function for the three stated outputs of the individual stack elements.

Because the synthesis system currently wires all drivers of a signal together, and we chose not to model conflict resolution. True resolution is not performed in the system simulation, instead, a simple logical OR function was implemented.

There are several other miscellaneous definitions in the package that serve as general utility definitions for the 2910 design project. A close examination of this package should give you ideas on what might be appropriate to include in other design project packages.

```
use work.SYNOPSYS.all;
package AMD_PACK is
```

Address bus is 12 bits wide

```
subtype ADDRESS_SIZE is INTEGER range 1 to 12;

subtype ADDRESS is UNSIGNED (ADDRESS_SIZE);

type ADDRESS_VECTOR is
    array (INTEGER RANGE<>) of ADDRESS;

type INSTRUCTION_OPS is (JZ, CJS, JMAP, CJP,
    PUSH, JSRP, CJV, JRP, RFCT, RPCT, CRTN,
    CJPP, LDCT, LOP, CONT, TWB);
```

16 instructions

```vhdl
type STACK_OPS is (S_NOOP, S_CLEAR,S_POP,
    S_PUSH);

subtype STACK_VECTOR_SIZE is POSITIVE range 1 to 9;

subtype STACK_VECTOR is BIT_VECTOR
    (STACK_VECTOR_SIZE);

type REGCNT_OPS is (NOOP, LOAD, DEC);
type UPC_OPS is (CLEAR, COUNT);

type Y_MUX_OPS is (SELECT_DATA,
    SELECT_REGCNT, SELECT_UPC,
    SELECT_STACK, SELECT_NONE);

-- Simulation specific functions

function HEX_TO_OP_CODE(HEX_VALUE : UNSIGNED
    (0 to 3))  return INSTRUCTION_OPS;

function WIRED_OR(SOURCES: BIT_VECTOR) return bit;

function WIRED_OR(SOURCES: ADDRESS_VECTOR)
    return ADDRESS;

end AMD_PACK;


package body AMD_PACK is
```

```vhdl
function HEX_TO_OP_CODE(HEX_VALUE : UNSIGNED
    (0 to 3))
    return INSTRUCTION_OPS is
begin
  case HEX_VALUE is
    when X"0" => return JZ;
    when X"1" => return CJS;
    when X"2" => return JMAP;
    when X"3" => return CJP;
    when X"4" => return PUSH;
    when X"5" => return JSRP;
    when X"6" => return CJV;
    when X"7" => return JRP;
    when X"8" => return RFCT;
    when X"9" => return RPCT;
    when X"a" => return CRTN;
    when X"b" => return CJPP;
    when X"c" => return LDCT;
    when X"d" => return LOP;
    when X"e" => return CONT;
    when X"f" => return TWB;
  end case;
end HEX_TO_OP_CODE;


function WIRED_OR(SOURCES: ADDRESS_VECTOR)
return ADDRESS is
    variable RESOLVED_ADDRESS : ADDRESS;
```

```vhdl
begin
  for BIT_INDEX in ADDRESS'LOW to ADDRESS'HIGH
loop
    RESOLVED_ADDRESS(BIT_INDEX) := '0';
    for WORD_INDEX in SOURCES'LEFT to
        SOURCES'RIGHT loop
      if(SOURCES(WORD_INDEX)(BIT_INDEX) = '1')
then
```

```
then
        RESOLVED_ADDRESS(BIT_INDEX) := '1';
     end if;
    end loop;
   end loop;
   return RESOLVED_ADDRESS;
  end WIRED_OR;

  function WIRED_OR( SOURCES: BIT_VECTOR) return BIT is
  begin
   for I in SOURCES'LEFT to SOURCES'RIGHT LOOP
    if SOURCES(I) = '1' then return '1'; end if;
   end loop;
   return '0';
  end WIRED_OR;

end AMD_PACK;
```

7

Reverse Synthesis

This chapter is a brief introduction to the reverse synthesis capability of the Design Compiler. After reading this chapter, you should have a basic understanding of the steps involved in the reverse synthesis process.

RoundTrip Synthesis

Reverse Synthesis Procedure

VHDL Netlist

Technology Independent VHDL

Reprocurement

RoundTrip Synthesis

RoundTrip Synthesis embodies the top-down synthesis process and the bottom-up synthesis process. These two capabilities combined yield a mechanism that has multiple uses. A tool with RoundTrip Synthesis capability that can read and write multiple design languages serves as a design gateway for migration between design environments. RoundTrip Synthesis provides level shifting in the abstraction hierarchy which can be used to translate between languages that have disparate abstraction capabilities (e.g., EDIF and VHDL).

Migration of existing designs into the VHDL design environment is a problem for all new adopters of VHDL, but RoundTrip Synthesis provides the automation necessary to ease the burden of the migration task. As will be shown in this chapter, RoundTrip Synthesis can be applied to the reprocurement problem faced by the DoD. Another novel use of RoundTrip Synthesis is the ability to always maintain functionally consistent models between levels of abstraction (technology independent or technology dependent); no matter which level of abstraction the design changes are most easily performed, Round-Trip Synthesis can generate the corresponding representation in the alternate level of abstraction.

RoundTrip Synthesis Model

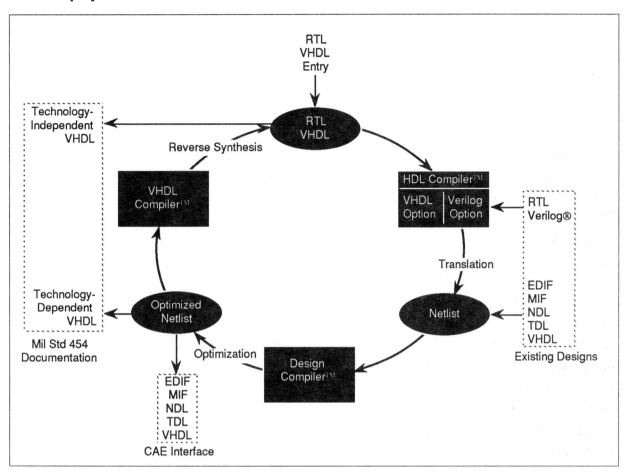

The Reverse Synthesis Procedure

Synopsys tools have the capability to take existing gate-level netlists and generate two different levels of VHDL descriptions. These two descriptions satisfy the network description requirements of MIL-STD 454L. The first VHDL description that can be generated is a VHDL netlist; it is generated via a netlist-to-netlist translation procedure. The second level of VHDL description generated is a technology-independent representation, using the data flow constructs of VHDL; for the case of a state machine, an RTL level description can be generated. The process of generating the technology-independent description from a technology-dependent netlist is called reverse synthesis.

The input to the reverse synthesis process is a gate-level netlist. Synopsys tools can read a variety of netlist formats including EDIF 2.0 (netlist and schematic), TDL, Verilog, NDL, VHDL, etc. First you use the read command to get the design into the system.

```
read -f edif BUS_ARB.edif
```

We have shown reading in an EDIF 2.0 netlist using a 1.5 micron CMOS technology for a bus arbitration network that is the target of the reverse synthesis process.

Next, we examine the gate level structure of the design before proceeding. This is a two step process; the schematic is generated and then viewed.

```
gen
view
```

The schematic may also be plotted to any postscript printer using the plot command.

To save the VHDL netlist, in the exact cell structure of the input network, the write command is used.

```
write -f vhdl -o BUS_ARB_GATES.vhd
```

The user can specify the relevant states of the machine and give them names to be used in the RTL level VHDL. This is especially valuable when not all of the 2 to the N possible states are used. Performing this step tells the tool which states are of interest so that it can take advantage of the don't care states, and produces more read-

able output.

```
set_fsm_encoding( {"Grant_A=001",  "Wait_A=011",  \
        "Timeout_A1=111", "Grant_B=010"  , \
        "Wait_B=110",   "Timeout_B1=101"} )
```

The next step is to tell the tool the order of the state vector. This tells the tool how to associate the state elements in the input netlist with the state encoding that was specified with the set_fsm_encoding command.

```
set_fsm_state_vector ( {FF2, FF1, FF0} );
```

Now the extract command can be used to generate an internal state table representation of the network.

```
extract
```

The last step is to create the RTL level VHDL for our state machine. This is accomplished using the write command.

```
write -f vhdl -o BUS_ARB_RTL.vhd
```

At this point we have completed the reverse synthesis process. We have taken the EDIF netlist for our bus arbitration network and generated its schematic. A VHDL netlist was generated, followed by an RTL level VHDL description. The entire process for this example takes less than five minutes.

Reverse Synthesis Source

The lengthy EDIF 2.0 source has not been
included; however, below we show the
automatically generated schematic for this
design.

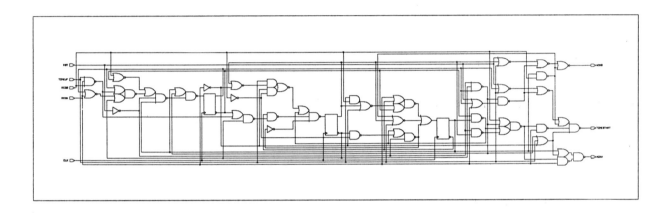

VHDL Netlist

The technology dependent VHDL netlist uses only the structural elements of VHDL. Note the introduction of signals to tie the design ports to the instances of the technology library gates. This listing shows the output of the Design Compiler netlist to netlist translation capability.

```
entity BUS_ARBITRATOR is

  port( REQA : in bit;  REQB : in bit;  TIMEUP : in bit;
        CLK : in bit;
     RST : in bit;  ACKA : out bit;  ACKB : out bit;
        TIMESTART : out bit);

end BUS_ARBITRATOR;

architecture STRUCTURAL_VIEW of BUS_ARBITRATOR is
  component AO4
    port( A : in bit;  B : in bit;  C : in bit;  D : in bit;  Z
        : out bit);
  end component;

  component AO7
    port( A : in bit;  B : in bit;  C : in bit;  Z : out bit);
  end component;

  component NR2
    port( A : in bit;  B : in bit;  Z : out bit);
  end component;

  component NR3
    port( A : in bit;  B : in bit;  C : in bit;  Z : out bit);
  end component;

  component ND2
```

```
    port( A : in bit;  B : in bit;  Z : out bit);
  end component;

  component ND3
    port( A : in bit;  B : in bit;  C : in bit;  Z : out bit);
  end component;

  component EON1
    port( A : in bit;  B : in bit;  C : in bit;  D : in bit;  Z
        : out bit);
  end component;

  component FD1
    port( D : in bit;  CP : in bit;  Q : out bit;  QN : out bit);
  end component;

  component OR3
    port( A : in bit;  B : in bit;  C : in bit;  Z : out bit);
  end component;

  component AO1
    port( A : in bit;  B : in bit;  C : in bit;  D : in bit;  Z
        : out bit);
  end component;

  component AO2
    port( A : in bit;  B : in bit;  C : in bit;  D : in bit;  Z
        : out bit);
  end component;

  component IVP
    port( A : in bit;  Z : out bit);
  end component;

  component AO3
    port( A : in bit;  B : in bit;  C : in bit;  D : in bit;  Z
        : out bit);
  end component;
```

```vhdl
signal TIMEUP_net, ACKA_net, ACKB_net, CLK_net,
    NET69, TIMESTART_net,
    NET67, NET65, NEXT_STATE_0, NEXT_STATE_1,
    NEXT_STATE_2, RST_net,
    CELL61_N50, CELL61_N51, CELL61_N52,
    CELL61_N53, CELL61_N40,
    CELL61_N41, CELL61_N54, CELL61_N55,
    CELL61_N42, CELL61_N43,
    CELL61_N56, CELL61_N44, CELL61_N31,
    CELL61_N45, CELL61_N46,
    CELL61_N34, CELL61_N47, CELL61_N35,
    CELL61_N48, PRESENT_STATE_0,
    CELL61_N36, CELL61_N49, CELL61_N23,
    PRESENT_STATE_1, CELL61_N37,
    PRESENT_STATE_2, CELL61_N24, REQB_net,
    CELL61_N38, CELL61_N25,
    REQA_net, CELL61_N39, CELL61_N26,
    CELL61_N27, CELL61_N28,
    CELL61_N29 : bit;

begin

    REQA_net <= REQA;
    REQB_net <= REQB;
    TIMEUP_net <= TIMEUP;
    CLK_net <= CLK;
    RST_net <= RST;
    ACKA <= ACKA_net;
    ACKB <= ACKB_net;
    TIMESTART <= TIMESTART_net;

    U7 : ND2  port map( A => PRESENT_STATE_2,
        B => CELL61_N29, Z => CELL61_N49);
    U8 : OR3  port map( A => TIMEUP_net,
        B => CELL61_N42,
        C => CELL61_N36, Z => CELL61_N47);
    U9 : NR2  port map( A => CELL61_N40, B =>
        CELL61_N50, Z => ACKB_net );

    U30 : AO2  port map( A => CELL61_N31,
        B => CELL61_N36, C => CELL61_N37,
        D => TIMEUP_net, Z => CELL61_N23);
    U31 : AO4  port map( A => CELL61_N42,
        B => REQB_net, C => CELL61_N49,
        D => CELL61_N24, Z => CELL61_N48);
    U32 : NR2  port map( A => CELL61_N36,
        B => PRESENT_STATE_2, Z => CELL61_N37);
    U20 : ND2  port map( A => CELL61_N34,
        B => NET67, Z=> CELL61_N25);
    U33 : OR3  port map( A => CELL61_N39,
        B => CELL61_N38, C => CELL61_N27,
        Z => NEXT_STATE_1);
    U21 : ND2  port map( A => REQA_net,
        B => CELL61_N48, Z => CELL61_N55);
    U34 : NR3  port map( A => PRESENT_STATE_2,
        B => _N40,
        C =>  TIMEUP_net, Z => CELL61_N39);
    U22 : NR2  port map( A => REQA_net,
        B => PRESENT_STATE_0, Z => CELL61_N46);
    U35 : ND2  port map( A => REQB_net,
        B => PRESENT_STATE_1, Z => CELL61_N40);
    U10 : NR2  port map( A => CELL61_N52,
        B => CELL61_N51, Z => CELL61_N50);
    U23 : AO7  port map( A => CELL61_N35,
        B => NET65, C => NET69, Z => CELL61_N34);
    U36 : IVP  port map( A => CELL61_N27,
        Z => CELL61_N26);
    U11 : AO4  port map( A => NET67, B => REQA_net,
        C => NET65, D => CELL61_N41,
        Z => CELL61_N38);
    U24 : NR2  port map( A => CELL61_N52,
        B => CELL61_N56, Z => CELL61_N54);
    FF0 : FD1  port map( D => NEXT_STATE_0,
        CP => CLK_net,
        Q =>  PRESENT_STATE_0, QN => NET65);
    U12 : ND2  port map( A => CELL61_N53,
        B => CELL61_N42, Z => CELL61_N52);
```

U25 : NR2 port map(A => NET65, B => REQB_net,
        Z => CELL61_N44);
FF1 : FD1 port map(D => NEXT_STATE_1,
        CP => CLK_net,
        Q => PRESENT_STATE_1, QN => NET67);
U13 : AO1 port map(A => REQB_net,
        B => _net, C => PRESENT_STATE_2,
        D => CELL61_N36, Z => CELL61_N41);
U26 : ND3 port map(A => REQA_net,
        B => TIMEUP_net, C => REQB_net,
        Z=> CELL61_N35);
FF2 : FD1 port map(D => NEXT_STATE_2,
        CP => CLK_net,
        Q => PRESENT_STATE_2, QN => NET69);
U14 : OR3 port map(A => PRESENT_STATE_0,
        B => _net, C => REQA_net, Z => CELL61_N53);
U27 : ND3 port map(A => NET69, B => CELL61_N29,
        C => PRESENT_STATE_0, Z => CELL61_N42);
U15 : AO7 port map(A => CELL61_N42,
        B => PRESENT_STATE_1, C => CELL61_N43,
        Z => NEXT_STATE_0);
U28 : IVP port map(A => REQA_net,
        Z => CELL61_N36);
U16 : NR3 port map(A => PRESENT_STATE_2,
        B => RST_net, C => TIMEUP_net,
        Z => CELL61_N51);
U29 : EON1 port map(A => CELL61_N47,
        B => PRESENT_STATE_1,
        C => REQA_net, D => CELL61_N48,
        Z => ACKA_net);
U17 : AO3 port map(A => CELL61_N45,
        B => CELL61_N44, C => CELL61_N29,
        D => PRESENT_STATE_1, Z => CELL61_N43);
U18 : AO3 port map(A => CELL61_N40,
        B => CELL61_N54, C => CELL61_N55,
        D => CELL61_N47, Z => TIMESTART_net);

U19 : AO4 port map(A => CELL61_N35,
        B => PRESENT_STATE_0, C => NET69,
        D => CELL61_N46, Z => CELL61_N45);
U0 : AO7 port map(A => CELL61_N28,
        B => CELL61_N24, C => CELL61_N29,
        Z => CELL61_N27);
U1 : IVP port map(A => RST_net, Z => CELL61_N29);
U2 : ND2 port map(A => CELL61_N31, B => NET69,
        Z => CELL61_N28);
U3 : IVP port map(A => REQB_net,
        Z => CELL61_N31);
U4 : ND2 port map(A => PRESENT_STATE_1,
        B => NET65, Z => CELL61_N24);
U5 : AO3 port map(A => CELL61_N24,
        B => CELL61_N23, C => CELL61_N25,
        D => CELL61_N26, Z => NEXT_STATE_2);
U6 : NR3 port map(A => PRESENT_STATE_0,
        B => RST_net, C => TIMEUP_net,
        Z => CELL61_N56);

end STRUCTURAL_VIEW;

Technology Independent VHDL

The RTL level VHDL generated for the state machine example is shown below. Note the use of the wait statement to infer the sequential behavior, and the usage of language constructs such as case, when, and if.

```
entity BUS_ARBITRATOR is
  port( CLK : in bit; REQA : in bit; REQB : in bit; TIMEUP :
      in bit;
      RST : in bit; ACKA : out bit; ACKB : out bit;
      TIMESTART
      : out bit);

end BUS_ARBITRATOR;

architecture STATE_MACHINE_VIEW of BUS_ARBITRATOR
      is
  type STATE_TYPE is ( Grant_A, Wait_A, Timeout_A1,
      Grant_B, Wait_B, Timeout_B1);

  signal STATE : STATE_TYPE;
  signal NEXT_STATE : STATE_TYPE;

begin
  -- This process waits for a clock edge before proceeding
  -- to the next state.
  SET_STATE: process
  begin
    wait until (not CLK'STABLE and CLK = '1');
    STATE <= NEXT_STATE;
  end process SET_STATE;

  -- This process determines the next state and output values
  -- based on the current state and input values.
  SET_NEXT_STATE: process (STATE, REQA, REQB,
TIMEUP, RST)
  begin
    case STATE is
```

```
when Grant_A =>
  if ((REQA and not(TIMEUP) and not(RST)) = '1')
        then
      ACKA <= '1';
      ACKB <= '0';
      TIMESTART <= '1';
      NEXT_STATE <= Grant_A;
  end if;
  if ((REQA and not(REQB) and not(RST)) = '1') then
      ACKA <= '1';
      ACKB <= '0';
      TIMESTART <= '1';
      NEXT_STATE <= Grant_A;
  end if;
  if ((REQA and REQB and TIMEUP and not(RST))
      = '1') then
      ACKA <= '0';
      ACKB <= '0';
      TIMESTART <= '0';
      NEXT_STATE <= Timeout_A1;
  end if;
  if ((not(REQA) and not(RST)) = '1') then
      ACKA <= '0';
      ACKB <= '0';
      TIMESTART <= '0';
      NEXT_STATE <= Wait_A;
  end if;
when Wait_A =>
  if ((REQA and not(REQB) and not(RST)) = '1') then
      ACKA <= '1';
      ACKB <= '0';
      TIMESTART <= '1';
      NEXT_STATE <= Grant_A;
  end if;
  if ((REQB and not(TIMEUP) and not(RST)) = '1')
        then
      ACKA <= '0';
      ACKB <= '1';
```

```vhdl
      TIMESTART <= '1';
      NEXT_STATE <= Grant_B;
    end if;
    if ((REQB and TIMEUP and not(RST)) = '1') then
      ACKA <= '0';
      ACKB <= '1';
      TIMESTART <= '1';
      NEXT_STATE <= Grant_B;
    end if;
    if ((not(REQA) and REQB and not(RST)) = '1') then
      ACKA <= '0';
      ACKB <= '1';
      TIMESTART <= '1';
      NEXT_STATE <= Grant_B;
    end if;
    if ((not(REQA) and not(REQB) and not(RST) ) = '1')
            then
      ACKA <= '0';
      ACKB <= '0';
      TIMESTART <= '0';
      NEXT_STATE <= Wait_A;
    end if;
  when Timeout_A1 =>
    if ((not(RST)) = '1') then
      ACKA <= '0';
      ACKB <= '0';
      TIMESTART <= '0';
      NEXT_STATE <= Wait_A;
    end if;
    if ((not(REQA) and not(REQB) and not(RST)) = '1')
            then
      ACKA <= '0';
      ACKB <= '0';
      TIMESTART <= '0';
      NEXT_STATE <= Wait_A;
    end if;
    if ((not(REQA) and REQB and not(RST)) = '1') then
      ACKA <= '0';

      NEXT_STATE <= Wait_A;
    end if;
  when Grant_B =>
    if ((REQB and not(TIMEUP) and not(RST)) = '1')
            then
      ACKA <= '0';
      ACKB <= '1';
      TIMESTART <= '1';
      NEXT_STATE <= Grant_B;
    end if;
    if ((not(REQA) and REQB and not(RST)) = '1')
            then
      ACKA <= '0';
      ACKB <= '1';
      TIMESTART <= '1';
      NEXT_STATE <= Grant_B;
    end if;
    if ((REQA and REQB and TIMEUP and not(RST))
       = '1') then
      ACKA <= '0';
      ACKB <= '0';
      TIMESTART <= '0';
      NEXT_STATE <= Timeout_B1;
    end if;
    if ((not(REQB)) = '1') then
      ACKA <= '0';
      ACKB <= '0';
      TIMESTART <= '0';
      NEXT_STATE <= Wait_B;
    end if;
    if ((not(REQA) and not(REQB)) = '1') then
      ACKA <= '0';
      ACKB <= '0';
      TIMESTART <= '0';
      NEXT_STATE <= Wait_B;
    end if;
  when Wait_B =>
    if ((REQA and not(RST)) = '1') then
```

```vhdl
        ACKA <= '1';
        ACKB <= '0';
        TIMESTART <= '1';
        NEXT_STATE <= Grant_A;
      end if;
      if ((not(REQA) and REQB and not(RST)) = '1') then
        ACKA <= '0';
        ACKB <= '1';
        TIMESTART <= '1';
        NEXT_STATE <= Grant_B;
      end if;
      if ((not(REQA) and not(REQB)) = '1') then
        ACKA <= '0';
        ACKB <= '0';
        TIMESTART <= '0';
        NEXT_STATE <= Wait_B;
      end if;
    when Timeout_B1 =>
      ACKA <= '0';
      ACKB <= '0';
      TIMESTART <= '0';
      NEXT_STATE <= Wait_B;
  end case;
 end process SET_NEXT_STATE;

end STATE_MACHINE_VIEW;
```

Reprocurement

The DoD has mandated the use of VHDL, primarily, to address the reprocurement problem that it faces for digital electronics. Major programs in the DoD span eight years from inception to production. In today's environment of rapidly changing technology, eight years represents three to four generations of integrated circuit technology. This means that any parts designed into one of the major programs will be obsolete before production begins.

Obsolescence is a problem from at least two standpoints. The first point is that newer technologies are more and more reliable, which extends the mean time before failure (MTBF); so, obsolete parts do not give a system its maximum reliability that is especially important in critical defense applications. The second problem with using obsolete parts in large systems is where to get them; a diminishing manufacturing source (DMS) is a severe problem. Silicon vendors typically do not continue to maintain process lines of more than three generations of technology at a time. This means that the source for many parts will disappear before the useful life of a particular program is over.

The present mode of operation by the DoD is to make "lifetime buys" of parts during their manufacturing lifetime. This means that the DoD will try to buy as many parts as it thinks it will need to build and maintain all of the serviceable systems. This is in complete opposition to the economic efficiency of a just-in-time manufacturing inventory discipline.

VHDL addresses the economic inefficiencies of the lifetime buy strategy by providing sufficient documentation to re-engineer a part in a currently available technology. When coupled with synthesis, VHDL provides an automated solution to the reprocurement problem. The existing design description is taken through the reverse synthesis process to produce a technology independent design (which is written in VHDL for technology independent design archival). That description is then used as the source for the synthesis process that will target a new technology, following which a new technology dependent VHDL description is written.

Two critical technical issues that need to be addressed in the automated reprocurement process. The first issue is design hierarchy. Hierarchy is important in that it provides a link between the design description in the old and the new technology; thus it is desirable to maintain. However, maintenence of hierarchy constrains the optimization process, so a balance is required. The user of reprocurement automation tools should be provided with sufficient hierarchy manipulation capability to arrive at an appropriate trade-off.

The second critical technical issue in automated reprocurement is timing. Often there is insufficient chip and system documentation to determine whether or not a faster (or slower for that matter) chip will work in the system. In these cases, the only recourse is to match the old chip's timing. This means that the synthesis tool used should have both minimum and maximum path delay optimization capabilities so that old path timings can be matched.

Synopsys worked with the Rockwell International Autonetics Electronics Systems Division and SMALC/MMETM group at McClellan Air Force Base to obtain an actual part cited for reprocurement. The original project was funded to show how VHDL could be used in the reprocurement process. The project involved the manual translation of the design netlist from a CAE workstation into a technology independent VHDL description, and the subsequent manual synthesis into the new target technology. The successful completion of this process required 40 man-weeks.

The goal of the follow on process was to mimic the manual path using the design automation provided by RoundTrip Synthesis. The chip is a part of the digital signal transfer unit (DSTU) card in the avionics of an F-111. The starting point for the Synopsys tool set was a VHDL structural model in a CMOS technology. The architecture of this chip is shown at right.

Digital Signal Transfer Unit Architecture

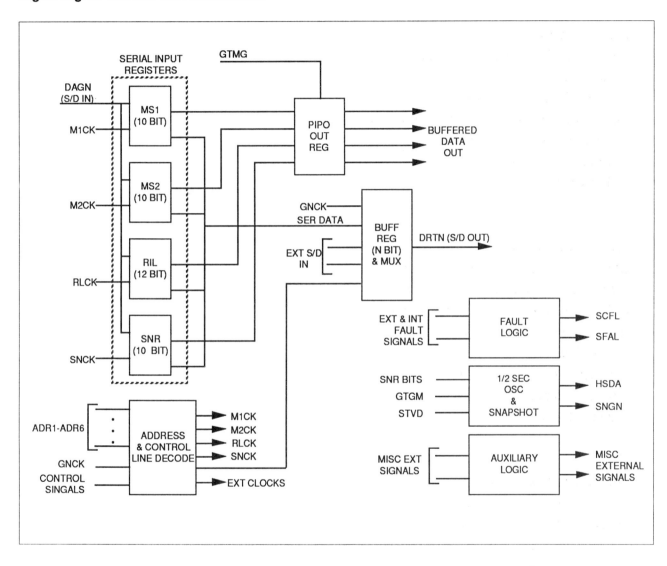

The first step was the creation of the technology independent VHDL description which was written out as part of the design documentation package. The decision was made to maintain the first two levels of hierarchy in the design. This allowed the optimization tools sufficient flexibility, while maintaining the overall design structure.

The second step was the retarget of the technology independent description into another CMOS technology. The resultant design description was then optimized several times, while maintaining the preserved design hierarchy, to experiment with the speed and area trade-off capabilites in the synthesis tools. The final netlists were also written out in VHDL format to complete the design portion of the documentation package.

The entire process, completed by an applications engineer with no design knowledge required less than one man-week of effort, including multiple implementations created by the synthesis capability, and including a project report. The automated path took one fortieth of the time of the manual effort. This remarkable achievement is made possible by RoundTrip Synthesis. A summary of the results has been included at right.

DSTU Chip Optimization Summary

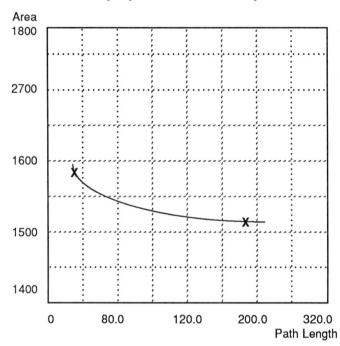

Call for Examples and Ideas

Synopsys plans a third edition of this work and you can participate. Please submit your ideas, design examples and comments to the author at:

> Synopsys Inc.
> 700 East Middlefield Road
> Mountain View, CA 94043-4033